THE ONLY ONE IN THE ROOM

How to Transform Differences into Strengths, Communicate With Impact, and Lead With Confidence

DENISE M. THOMAS

The Effective Communication Coach

I dedicate this book to those who came after me — my amazing children, Dominique and Daren. It's also for those who came before me — Elijah Junior and Maurene Thomas, Elijah Senior and Essie B. Thomas, George and Agatha Schroeder, and all my ancestors — whose strength runs through my veins.

Most of all, it's for those who walk with me now, lighting the path forward with love and truth.

Copyright © 2025 Denise M. Thomas
Cover & Layout Design: Mel Wise

All rights reserved. No part of this book may be reproduced, distributed, or transmitted in any form or by any means, including photocopying, recording, scanning, or other electronic or mechanical methods, without the prior written permission of the copyright holder, except in the case of brief quotations embodied in critical reviews and certain other noncommercial uses permitted by copyright law.

Prohibition of AI Training:
This book and its contents, including but not limited to text, images, and design elements, are expressly prohibited from being used to train, develop, or improve any artificial intelligence (AI) systems, machine learning models, or similar technologies without the explicit written consent of the copyright holder. Unauthorized use for such purposes constitutes a violation of the author's intellectual property rights.

Uploading or distributing photos, scans, or any content from this book without prior permission is theft of the author's intellectual property. Please honor the author's work as you would your own.

Thank you in advance for respecting the author's rights.

The Only One in the Room: How to Transform Differences into Strengths, Communicate With Impact, and Lead With Confidence

ISBN Hardcover: 978-1-940498-48-5
ISBN Paperback: 978-1-940498-47-8
ISBN eBook: 978-1-940498-49-2

Contents

Foreword — vii
Introduction — 1

PART 1: CULTURE WINS EVERY TIME — 17
Chapter 1: Culture Eats Strategy for Breakfast — 21
Chapter 2: The Hidden Costs of Culture Misalignment — 49

PART 2: OWN YOUR DIFFERENCE — 65
Chapter 3: Are you Fitting In or Belonging? — 69
Chapter 4: Unleashing Your Signature Communication Style — 87

PART 3: MAKING EVERYONE MATTER — 125
Chapter 5: Start Where You Are — 127
Chapter 6: Moving in the Right Direction — 147

PART 4: DRIVING BREAKTHROUGH TRANSFORMATION — 183
Chapter 7: The Social Capitalist — 185
Chapter 8: Are we Winning or Dominating? — 207

PART 5: THE FUTURE OF ORGANIZATIONAL COMMUNICATION — 235
Chapter 9: Sustainability and Resilience — 237
Chapter 10: Your Dash — 259
Conclusion: Your Voice Your Legacy — 271
About the Author — 275

Foreword

I'll never forget the day I first met Denise Thomas. We were in Chicago, sharing the stage at a mutual client event where she was serving as the emcee for the day in addition to delivering a powerful presentation of her own.

I was immediately struck by Denise's persona and presence. She wasn't just emceeing or presenting, she was connecting. She wasn't just polished; she was real. Her authenticity, her message, and her voice were unmistakable. There was something in the way her insights, clarity, and warmth inspired the room and had people listening intently.

When she finished the day, I remember turning to her and saying, "You're remarkable, you've got an amazing book in you, and the world needs it."

I also told her that when she wrote this book that I'd write the foreword.

Well, she's written it! And you're holding it in your hands or listening to it in your ears.

The Only One in the Room is not only a terrific book about communication, it's also an invaluable field guide for navigating leadership, difference, and authenticity in a world that too often rewards conformity and punishes individuality. Denise understands, in both her mind and heart, as well as through experience, that being "the only one in the room" isn't just an identity; it's also an opportunity. And through this timely book, she not only gives us the courage to own it, but also the framework, language, and process to transform that uniqueness into our leadership superpower.

What Denise offers here is both profoundly personal and immediately practical. You'll find tools and strategies grounded in decades of experience, both hers and those of the many professionals and organizations she's helped. But even more than that, you'll find wisdom and heart. She doesn't tell us to work harder to fit in; instead, she teaches us how to stand out by being fully ourselves.

She challenges us to reframe what we once saw as liabilities — our difference, our doubts, our discomfort — and to see them instead as advantages, as signals of value, as proof that we bring something unique. As Denise says, "You're not powerless." That truthful message is a lifeline to so many. In this sense, *The Only One in the Room* is a call to lead with trust and to live with courage. It's about owning our voice and using it to elevate not just ourselves but the people around us.

You'll also be introduced to Denise's *Owning the Room Communication Roadmap*, a guide that turns invisible labor into visible impact. You'll see how leaders can use communication to ignite culture, how emerging talent can use it to accelerate influence, and how communicating our differences effectively can become a strength.

For me, what makes Denise's work so relevant and valuable today is how deeply it aligns with the core principles I champion in my book, *Trust and Inspire.* She shows us that leadership is not about controlling others or merely conforming to norms. Instead, leadership is about seeing, developing and unleashing potential in ourselves and others. Her framework invites us to lead by modeling authenticity, communicating with purpose, and building cultures of trust and belonging. And when that communication is rooted in authenticity, it becomes transformative for everyone involved.

Throughout these pages, you'll find practical tools grounded in research and real-world application. You'll meet the "Jordan" in every organization, i.e., the contributor who is capable, committed, and often overlooked. Denise not only names the "Credit Gap," where some do the work while others take the credit, but she also teaches us how to close it, through intentional communication that reclaims voice, visibility, and value.

But what I admire most is that Denise does all this while staying grounded in humanity. She doesn't ask us to pretend or "to seem" but instead invites us to be real. To lead with transparency, vulnerability, and authenticity. To build relationships and trust, rather than seeking positional power. To speak so we are not just heard but also felt.

So, to every reader who's ever doubted if they belonged, or who's felt unseen or unheard, this book is for you. And to every leader who wants to better connect, inspire, and lead in today's diverse and dynamic world, this book is for you too.

Denise Thomas is who I thought she was: authentic, courageous, principled, the real deal. And *The Only One in the Room* is her invitation to all of us to be real as well.

I encourage you to read, apply, and share this book. Most of all, I hope the principles and applications you learn from it can help give you the permission and power to own your difference, and to unleash the superpower that's already inside you.

— Stephen M. R. Covey

The New York Times and #1 *Wall Street Journal* bestselling author of *The Speed of Trust* and *Trust and Inspire*

Introduction

Disclaimer: The stories and characters in this book draw from my personal experiences in the corporate world. While they reflect my genuine memories and perspectives, all names of individuals and organizations have been changed to protect privacy. The companies I reference as *Stonehaven*, *Ironwood*, and *Bedrock Solution*s are not intended to depict any single entity, but rather serve as composite representations of the corporate environments that influenced and shaped my professional journey.

Communication is just like money — it's a critical tool that determines whether you thrive or merely survive.

It's not a "soft skill."

I'll say that again, louder for the people in the back: Communication is not a soft skill.

It's not secondary.

It's not just what happens in big meetings or formal presentations.

Communication IS the currency that drives EVERY aspect of your professional success.

Wherever you are in your career, wherever you aspire to be, you need to understand how you can leverage communication. It's the number one skill that can move you toward your big personal development goals.

And for CEOs, business leaders, or company owners, the data is clear. Communication impacts your bottom line:

- Poor communication within the workplace costs U.S. companies an estimated $1.2 trillion annually.[1]
- Employees working in "High Trust Cultures" are 74% less stressed and 50% more productive.[2]
- Workplaces with effective communication strategies enjoy 4.5 times higher employee retention rates.[3]
- Effective leadership can reduce employee turnover by up to 32%.[4]

Given these statistics, let's do some quick, back-of-the-envelope math. For example, a company with 500 employees and a 20% turnover rate loses 100 employees annually.

100 employees x $50,000 (the estimated replacement cost) = $5 million per year in turnover costs.

According to Deloitte's 2025 *Human Capital Trends Report*, improving communication and leadership could reduce turnover by 32%, in this case, saving $1.6 million per year.[5]

The facts are undeniable, but the question remains: why do so many professionals and organizations treat communication as an afterthought rather than a strategic imperative?

Perhaps it's because the true cost of poor communication isn't always immediately visible on the balance sheet. Unlike equipment failures or supply chain disruptions, communication breakdowns create

---

[1] "15 Workplace Communication Statistics You Need to Know," *Sociable*, December 10, 2024 (https://www.sociabble.com/blog/employee-communications/communications-statistics).

[2] Paul J. Zak, "The Neuroscience of Trust," Harvard Business Review, January-February 2017 (https://hbr.org/2017/01/the-neuroscience-of-trust).

[3] "15 Workplace Communication Statistics You Need to Know," *Sociable*, December 10, 2024 (https://www.sociabble.com/blog/employee-communications/communications-statistics).

[4] Jason Flynn, et al, "Turning Tensions into Triumphs: Helping Leaders Transform Uncertainty into Opportunity," Deloitte's Human Capital Trends Report 2025, March 24, 2025 (https://www2.deloitte.com/us/en/insights/focus/human-capital-trends/2025/thriving-in-midst-leadership-tension-uncertainty.html).

[5] Jason Flynn, et al, "Turning Tensions into Triumphs: Helping Leaders Transform Uncertainty into Opportunity," *Deloitte's Human Capital Trends Report 2025*, March 24, 2025 (https://www2.deloitte.com/us/en/insights/focus/human-capital-trends/2025/thriving-in-midst-leadership-tension-uncertainty.html).

silent inefficiencies that compound over time, resulting in missed opportunities, fractured relationships, and talent drain that happens so gradually we barely notice until the damage is done.

Ask yourself: What would change if you invested in communication with the same intentionality you apply to improving your technical skills or hitting your quarterly sales targets? What possibilities might open up if your team could harness the full power of clear, authentic communication?

The math isn't just compelling. It's transformative. And in today's hyper-connected workplace, those who master this critical currency will define the future of work itself.

Communication: Your Untapped Superpower in the Workplace

Many of us have been socialized to believe that communication is something we only need to focus on when we're interviewing for a job, giving a high stakes presentation, or speaking from the stage. We are trained to think of communication as a means to an end. It's only valuable insofar as it can help us achieve immediate goals or create specific outcomes. We put a lot of pressure on ourselves to show up at our best in these moments. But what if we made communication more a part of our day-to-day standard operating procedure? What would change if we treated communication as a skill that's equally as crucial as our technical expertise or business acumen?

I'm here to tell you that your voice — how you use it, when you use it, and why you use it — is your most valuable asset... Let's not forget who's on the receiving end of your voice.

I spent over 20 years as an employee and leader navigating Fortune 100 companies like Bedrock Solutions, and Ironwood developing the ability to deliver and receive messages across language, culture, and communication-style barriers. Now I do the same for my clients as the Effective Communication Coach (realcommcoach.com). What I've learned is that technical proficiency gets you in the game, but your communication signature determines how far you'll go.

THE DAY I DISCOVERED MY SUPERPOWER

I'll never forget the moment I truly understood communication as currency. I was working at Stonehaven, where I'd been promoted from being a liaison between IT developers and end users to change management leader. My executive leader pulled me aside to give me what felt like an impossible assignment: present our new change management plan to the entire executive leadership team — VPs, directors, the whole C-suite.

"Denise, be you," he told me. "Everyone is going to expect this typical slide-heavy, data-driven presentation. But I'm choosing you because I know that within the scope of this change management project, people are very anxious. People have a lot of reservations. I'm putting my faith in you because I know you're going to do it in a way that people haven't heard before. I believe you will put them at ease and get them excited about what we're doing."

That moment introduced me to my gift: my ability to create connection rather than just deliver information. When I spoke to that room of executives, I wasn't focused on impressing them with perfect slides or flawless delivery. I focused on connecting with their concerns, their reality, their humanity.

I could see it happening in real time — the heads nodding, the eye contact, the shift in energy — as people leaned in rather than checked out. The presentation was an undeniable success. It was unanimously accepted and created momentum for the entire change management process.

That presentation also changed the trajectory of my career. After that meeting, I was asked to facilitate kickoff sessions for every brewery in our network. And I can directly connect the dots between that experience and founding the Effective Communication Coach (realcommcoach.com) years later. But even more importantly, it taught me something I now share with every client: there's going to be a day when something powerful happens, when people remember not just what you did, but what you said and how you made them feel. As Maya Angelou reminds us, "People will forget what you said, people will forget what you did, but people will never forget how you made them feel."

Communication is about creating connection through your words and inspiring others through your presence. From that moment on, I understood that effective communication isn't a soft skill. It's a critical skill. I started treating it like my career superpower, and it opened doors that no degree or credential ever could have

Let me be clear: performance is just the entry ticket — it won't take you to the next level. And in my work with leaders, I see too many brilliant people falling into what I call the Competence Trap. Professionals, who reach a high level in their careers because they have incredible technical skills, eventually hit a ceiling because they lack communication skills. The Competence Trap leads to other problems like the Credit Gap.

Picture this: You're sitting in the quarterly meeting when a colleague stands up and says, "I'm thrilled to deliver this project. Thanks to Jordan for her support..." Meanwhile, you know Jordan was an equal partner (or maybe even did most of the work) on the project.

Yeah, I see you nodding your head because you've been there.

We've all been there.

This scenario resonates either because you've been "Jordan" or you've known many "Jordans." Getting the credit you deserve is a constant battle. And by the way, this is true whether you're Black, white, Latinx, or Asian; a man, a woman, or non-binary; LGBTQ+ or straight; a veteran, a person with disabilities, white collar or blue collar; introverted or extraverted, neurodivergent, etc. The Credit Gap can affect anyone in any workplace.

While I wish I could wave a magic wand and make every human you work with aware of how it sounds when they say "thank you for your support" or "thank you for your help" in a situation where you played a leading role. I believe a better solution is to make YOU aware of what you can do to own your worth and close the Credit Gap. Let this book be your guide.

The end goal is no more waiting around for recognition and no more feeling paralyzed by fear or reservations about saying or doing the wrong thing. Being in the game for 20+ years, I've been able to navigate these experiences as both a high performer and as a CEO. Once you learn how to tap into communication as your superpower, you will be unstoppable.

The Only One in the Room

There's one thing the "Jordans" of the world have in common: they are often "the only one in the room." In other words, their difference leads to an "othering," being treated as a support person, and an experience of a lack of belonging. Being "the only one in the room" or the "black sheep" of the office or the person who feels like they don't belong — however you want to say it — is tough. Your job as you're reading this book is to discover YOUR VALUE being "the only one in the room".

That's right! Two things can be true at the same time: (a) it's difficult when your difference makes you feel like you don't belong and (b) there is value in your difference. Together, we're going to uncover that value.

It can be tough to ask for and receive full recognition of your brilliance when you feel like you need to be someone you're not just to fit in. You don't want to be labeled "too much" or "not enough." All you want is for someone to see you. It's like running a marathon while everyone else is walking. I get it. I've been there. And I'm here to tell you that you can reframe your difference and use your voice as your superpower. I promise.

Whenever you feel like you're "the only one in the room" from a communication and leadership standpoint, it's critical to understand how you got there.

This reality hit me powerfully when I was working as an intern at Bedrock Solutions. I was tasked with presenting to a room full of men working in manufacturing. When I walked in, I just felt this exhausting weight of being "the only one in the room". Let me paint the picture for you: Here I am, this young (I was 27), Black woman in a room full of 100 white guys. Also, we are in southern Indiana where I grew up — I'm probably the only person in the room who doesn't hunt or drink beer — and I was there to *train* them. Talk about feeling "othered"!

I remember preparing by getting to the plant extra early. Even before I started talking, the guys were leaning back with their arms crossed, looking me up and down. They did not roll out the welcome wagon. And I thought to myself, "Okay, I got this. I'm going to bring it. I'm going to make sure the next time you see me, you'll remember me, and the next time you see somebody else that looks like me, you won't have that same reaction."

Sure enough, I crushed it. I earned my stripes. And it made my brand as a communicator and coach even more powerful. My training got really good reviews, in part because I turned being "the only one in the room" to my advantage.

The lesson: You can either make a decision to let your difference be your kryptonite, or say, "Okay, I'm going to show y'all."

"Code-switching" and the "Adaptation Tax" are common terms used to describe what I'm talking about here: the exhausting work of constantly conforming to communication expectations that don't align with your natural strengths. Most often these terms have been applied to people belonging to non-dominant or marginalized groups. However, it's important to recognize that white men can also feel disconnected, disengaged, and undervalued in the workplace. Many well-intentioned members of the dominant social class, or simply the dominant group in a particular office setting, spend time worrying that something they say or do will offend someone else. All of these big feelings represent gaps that effective communication can bridge.

What happens when you're "the only one in the room" is complex and should be a high priority area of focus amongst professionals. When you don't communicate your value clearly, someone else will claim it. Your contributions will become invisible, and invisible work doesn't get rewarded. When you learn how to communicate in a way that shows people you own your worth — that you know you're "the only one in the room," and you're ready to flex it — that's when the sparks will fly (in a good way!).

THE ORGANIZATIONAL ADAPTATION TAX

This isn't just a personal career challenge, though. It also represents a major organizational liability. There's an Adaptation Tax paid by organizations too. Companies lose valuable insights when diverse perspectives go unvoiced. Innovation stalls when unique approaches are suppressed to make room for dominant norms. Employee engagement plummets when people feel they must constantly wear a mask to work. The resulting turnover costs, missed opportunities, and diminished performance directly impact the bottom line.

Organizations that recognize and address this communication gap build a significant competitive advantage through enhanced problem-solving, greater innovation, and stronger talent retention.

While I want organizations to take note and consider how they can change their cultures to reward all employees for the unique contributions they bring to the table, I also want individuals to take responsibility for the areas where they can step it up. In this book, we attack this problem from both perspectives.

I hope it's clear that I'm not trying to blame the victim here. I simply want you to know that you're not powerless. The great news is that you can learn some simple and effective communication strategies that change this dynamic completely. I haven't met anyone who was born with the ability to articulate their value. Fortunately for all of us, it's a skill you can develop with the ease of knowing there is no expiration date on the pursuit of excellence.

Throughout my career, I've seen professionals at every level transform how they're perceived and valued simply by changing how they communicate. I share many of their stories in the pages that follow. I'll also share the exact methods that have helped thousands of clients move from overlooked to indispensable, from silent to influential, from uncertain to confident. These aren't theoretical concepts. They're practical tools designed to ignite your feeling of belonging.

Who is This Book For?

Before we get to work, I want to set some expectations and provide you with the value proposition for this book. This is a key part of my coaching philosophy. I want us all to be on the same page from the jump.

For ambitious contributors who consistently deliver excellent work but wonder why others seem to advance faster, this book reveals how communication, not just performance, determines career trajectory. You'll gain the tools to make your contributions visible, build strategic relationships, and transform what feels like "otherness" into your greatest professional advantage.

For people managers caught between driving results and supporting their teams, this book provides the roadmap for doing both effectively. You'll learn to create psychological safety that actually improves performance, communicate change in ways that generate buy-in rather than resistance, and build the kind of team culture that attracts and retains top talent.

Regardless of your role or level, there's a common thread that connects every reader of this book. Every human being who picks up this book can relate to wanting to belong, regardless of position, title, or identity. Reader, I bet you've asked yourself at some point, maybe even today, "do I belong here?" This book is for ANYONE who has ever felt like THAT, like "the only one in the room," whether because of your background, age, abilities, race, gender, identity, or simply because your perspective differs from the dominant group at whatever table you're sitting at (e.g., single in an office full of partnered people with children).

It's for leaders struggling with employee engagement, change management, and building authentic connections in increasingly diverse workplaces.

It's for aspiring leaders who want to develop their voice before their authority is formally recognized.

It's for young professionals just getting started in their careers who want to learn how to communicate their value.

INTRODUCTION

I've built my career being the bridge between different worlds. My journey began when I entered life without a connection to my biological parents, adopted at five months old. My adoptive parents, with my mother's rich West Indian heritage and my father's traditional values, provided stability and beliefs that shaped my foundation. And I'm eternally grateful for the gifts they shared with me. My mother's Caribbean background brought a unique perspective to my upbringing, one that emphasized integrity, education, and resilience. But emotional expression wasn't exactly our family's language. Practical care and steady presence were how love was communicated. That early experience of abandonment by my birth parents, followed by being raised in an environment where, as I often say, "lunch was the love," shaped how I would communicate and connect with others throughout my life. In other words, being warm and welcoming with unfamiliar people didn't come naturally for me. I had to develop keen skills for reading people and situations. I learned how to pick up on subtle cues that others might miss.

When I entered the workforce, I was often "the only one in the room"—the only Black woman, the youngest, the only single parent. At first, I was outraged that anyone would make me feel "othered," though I quickly discovered that if I wanted to get ahead, I couldn't even come close to expressing that outrage. Instead, I learned to see my difference as my advantage and how to express that. As a Black woman who was used to being marginalized (e.g., experiencing microaggressions and biases), I took those toxic experiences and transformed them into powerful communication tools. As demonstrated by the personal stories I've already shared and the stories in the coming pages, I know what it feels like to be overlooked, so I developed the ability to ensure everyone at the table feels seen and heard. That superpower has served me well in any number of ways.

A Hollywood writer drafting a screenplay about my life, taking their cues from statistical probability, would have written a very different ending to my story. According to conventional predictions, based on my background and where I came from, I'm not supposed to be advising Fortune 100 executives, coaching leaders, or speaking around the world. Yet, here I am because I refuse to let my past define my journey. And this is a truth I want to share with you: Your circumstances don't determine your destination — your voice does.

How to Use this Book

Earlier I said I'm the Effective Communication Coach (realcommcoach.com). It's important that we get something straight from the outset: I see a big distinction between training and coaching. I'm a coach, not a trainer. Trainers try to instill and impose best practices on their trainees. Training is for animals at the zoo! What I do is very different. I bring out the best in people — the best that *already exists* inside my clients and inside of YOU.

Throughout these pages, I'll guide you to develop your own unique communication approach. We'll start by examining the broader organizational landscape, understanding how culture and strategy connect, recognizing dysfunction, and seeing where individuals like us often get caught in the crossfire. Then we'll narrow our focus to YOU: how to find and amplify your authentic voice within whatever organizational reality you're facing.

Whether you're in an organization that genuinely values different perspectives or one that's still stuck in old patterns, the principles we'll explore will serve you. If you're fortunate enough to work somewhere that recognizes when you feel valued you do better work, great! You can position yourself to rise within a progressive culture. If your current reality is more challenging, I'll share strategies for navigating those non-ideal scenarios while maintaining your integrity.

What you should know is that you don't have to stoop to anyone's level.

Be you.

Be proud.

And don't be afraid to rise above the fray.

As you read, you'll navigate *The Owning the Room Communication Roadmap* — a practical framework for moving from wherever you are now to where you want to be. You'll also encounter exercises to help you put this framework into action.

I've developed this roadmap over the course of the past 20+ years. But in the spirit of full transparency, when I first started coaching, one of my clients said that although their coaching sessions with me were good, they had a hard time implementing what they learned. In response, I developed different ways to measure and communicate progress to clients. *The Owning the Room Communication Roadmap* is how I'm incorporating that client insight.

I've packed this book with real-world examples from my own personal experiences and from my actual client work alongside evidence-based research. While I've changed the names and some identifying details to protect privacy, all the lessons I share have been tried and tested through genuine situations I've witnessed. These aren't hypotheticals or made-up case studies from business school textbooks — they're real challenges faced by real leaders and the solutions that actually moved the needle.

In Part 1, we'll kick things off by examining "The Culture-Strategy Connection," exploring why even brilliant strategic plans fail when they're not supported by strong communication cultures.

>  **TRUTH BOMB**
>
> Did you know organizations with poor communication practices experience higher employee turnover rates[6] and as much as 25% lower productivity?[7] Communication isn't a nice-to-have. It's a competitive advantage.

Note:  **Truth Bomb** *boxes will be provided throughout the book to highlight key insights. These "Truth Bomb" are designed to cut through the noise and deliver powerful, actionable wisdom in a direct way. Think of them as the statements I'd emphasize if we were speaking face-to-face. They're the kind of insights that might make you pause, reflect, or even take notes (which I encourage you to do!). They represent the core principles that have transformed my clients' approaches to communication and leadership. Don't skip these. They're the concentrated essence of what makes this approach work.*

Note: 🕐 **Time Out** *boxes will be provided throughout the book. Think of them as deliberate pauses in our conversation—moments when I'm asking you to step back from the rush of information and reflect. Sometimes they'll offer insight on a complex topic, other times they'll invite you to consider how a concept applies specifically to your situation. These are intentional opportunities to deepen your understanding and personalize your takeaways. Just as the most effective communicators know when to pause for impact, these boxes create space for the ideas to truly land before we move forward together.*

Part 2 focuses on "Finding Your Voice in a Changing Workplace." You'll discover your Unique Values and Capabilities (UVC) — the intersection of what you value and what you do exceptionally well. This section will help you figure out not only what makes you the best at what you do, but also how to communicate that to others. We'll also discuss techniques to help you stand out authentically in an increasingly AI-driven world.

---

6   Corey Tatel and Ben Wigert, "42% of Employee Turnover is Preventable but Often Ignored," *Gallup*, July 10, 2024 (https://www.gallup.com/workplace/646538/employee-turnover-preventable-often-ignored.aspx).

7   Michael Chui, et al, "The Social Economy: Unlocking Value and Productivity Through Social Technology," *McKinsey Global institute*, July 1, 2012 (https://www.mckinsey.com/industries/technology-media-and-telecommunications/our-insights/the-social-economy).

Aimed primarily at leaders reflecting on how to keep their teams performing at a high level, Part 3 guides you through "Igniting a Culture of Belonging," showing how the Three Pillars of transformative communication (transparency, vulnerability, and humanity) create environments where people thrive, not just survive. While senior leaders and executives can benefit from these chapters, it's even more important for aspiring leaders who want to understand how to position themselves for future advancement.

In Part 4, you'll learn about "Driving Breakthrough Transformation" by building what I call Social Capital: the relationships that determine whether your initiatives succeed or fail. We'll also explore how to measure communication return on investment (ROI) in ways that demonstrate tangible business impact. This is where we take out our measuring tools and get into the data. Forget about winning, let's focus on dominating.

Finally, Part 5 looks at "The Future of Organizational Communication," both from the perspective of leaders and from the standpoint of individual contributors. If we look at communication as currency, what can we do to build resilience and sustainability into your communication approach, and how can that support your legacy?

Whether you're a senior executive responsible for organizational transformation or an emerging professional looking to make your mark, the lessons in this book will translate directly to business results. I promise that I've seen these techniques work and with lightning speed. Many of the chapters include assessments and exercises so that you can put what you find most relevant and valuable to work and start seeing results immediately.

You'll learn to navigate the full spectrum of effective communication at work without going through the exhausting process of compromising who you truly are. This matters because when you show up authentically and communicate effectively, you don't just advance your own career — you transform the organizations you serve.

Remember: Your success is your company's success.

>  **TRUTH BOMB**
>
> Here's the number one takeaway: the greatness you're seeking is already inside you.
>
> Like at the end of *The Wizard of Oz* when Glinda "The Good Witch" says to Dorothy, "You've always had the power [to get back home], my dear. You had it all along," your power to transform your career and your organization through effective communication is already within you.
>
> My job isn't to teach you how to be great. It's to help you recognize and OWN the greatness that's already there.

This book is designed to be a part of your toolkit. It's designed to further elevate your leadership impact. Read this book as a blueprint and not a backup plan. You won't regret it!

Are you ready to leverage communication to own YOUR difference and unlock YOUR career superpower? Let's go.

PART 1
CULTURE WINS EVERY TIME

In the Introduction, I said communication is just like money — it's a critical tool that determines whether you thrive or merely survive. And yes, this applies to your teams and organizations just as much as it does to you as an individual.

Have you seen the numbers lately? They tell a sobering story, and it ain't pretty:

- A 2024 Gallup survey shows that the percentage of employees who strongly agree that their organization cares about their overall well-being has plunged from 49% in 2020 to 21% in 2024.[8]
- This isn't just an HR headache. We're talking about $8.9 trillion lost in global GDP from disengaged employees.[9]
- And here's what really stands out: when asked what would improve their work life, "quiet quitters" ranked workplace culture and well-being way above getting paid more.[10]

>  **TRUTH BOMB**
>
> People aren't leaving companies. They're leaving toxic cultures — and it's costing organizations billions.

---

[8] "Employee Well-being," *Gallup*, (https://www.gallup.com/394424/indicator-employee-well-being.aspx).

[9] "2024 State of the Global Workplace," *Gallup*, (https://www.gallup.com/workplace/349484/state-of-the-global-workplace.aspx#ite-506924).

[10] "2024 State of the Global Workplace," *Gallup*, (https://www.gallup.com/workplace/349484/state-of-the-global-workplace.aspx#ite-506924).

Let's be honest. We're facing a connection crisis in our workplaces. If you've ever felt like you don't quite belong, like your perspective isn't valued, or like you're constantly code-switching just to fit in, you're experiencing this crisis firsthand. The heart of the problem? That disconnect between your organization's culture and your strategic objectives.

But here's why this matters to you personally: When culture and strategy are misaligned, it's people like us — those who already feel different — who suffer the most. We become scapegoats when initiatives fail. Our ideas get dismissed more easily. We're asked to be "team players" while watching our contributions get minimized or overlooked entirely.

Understanding the culture-strategy connection gives you power. It helps you recognize when an organization's dysfunction isn't about your performance, but about their broken systems. More importantly, it positions you to become part of the solution rather than a casualty of the problem.

In Chapter 1, "Culture Eats Strategy for Breakfast," I'll show you the hard truth many leaders miss: brilliant strategies collect dust when they don't align with your company's cultural DNA. Think about it — no matter how meticulously you craft those initiatives, if your culture doesn't support them, they're dead on arrival.

For those of us who are often "the only one in the room," this knowledge becomes a survival tool. You'll learn to spot the difference between organizations that say they value diversity and those that actually create cultures where diverse perspectives can thrive. You'll discover how three key elements — transparency, vulnerability, and humanity — create the foundation where your unique contributions can actually be recognized and valued.

Then in Chapter 2, "The Hidden Costs of Cultural Misalignment," we'll dig deeper into what this disconnect really costs (not just organizations, but individuals like you). Beyond the obvious metrics like turnover and productivity drops, there are personal costs you might be absorbing: the mental energy you spend navigating dysfunction, the career opportunities lost when innovation gets stifled, and the "Adaptation Tax" I mentioned earlier. Stop for a moment and consider all that energy you waste trying to fit into broken systems instead of contributing your best work. It's staggering!

When diverse perspectives stay silent because the culture doesn't support them, everyone loses. And we must never forget that those perspectives belong to real people with real careers at stake. As the editorial team at *Women of Influence+* puts it: Organizations that claim to have a caring culture must align rhetoric with reality or face both external and internal consequences, including the exodus of talent that could have transformed their business.[11]

Understanding these dynamics helps you make strategic choices about where to invest your energy and talent. You've got to recognize organizations that either can't or won't change, and make your choices accordingly. As a wise mentor once told me, "Sometimes in order to elevate you must separate," which isn't about abandoning ship, but about making strategic choices about where you can actually thrive.

Here's the truth: when you understand how culture and strategy connect, you become equipped to help build environments where people like us don't just fit in, we stand out for all the right reasons.

---

11   "Is Your Company Truly Caring, or Just Carewashing?" *Women of Influence+*, September 11, 2024 (https://www.womenofinfluence.ca/2024/09/11/is-your-company-truly-caring-or-just-carewashing/#:~:text=It%20starts%20with%20aligning%20rhetoric%20with%20reality.,a%20culture%20of%20trust%20and%20psychological%20safety).

Chapter 1
Culture Eats Strategy for Breakfast

> "When two or more individuals come together,
> it's like there's a third person in the room. 'Culture'
> is the third person."
>
> – Fabiana Nardi, CultureTalk Certified Partner, DisruptHR Sao Paulo

Leadership offsites, strategic planning sessions, quarterly syncs, all-hands meetings — we've all been there, right? These rituals are supposed to keep your organization running smoothly. When they work, it feels almost magical. Strategies crystallize; leaders leave energized and ready to inspire their teams to action.

But here's the reality: all of it becomes wasted effort if your culture doesn't support the strategy.

Let me say that again because it's worth repeating: If the culture doesn't support the strategy, the strategy will fail. Period.

This isn't just my opinion. "Culture eats strategy for breakfast" is a phrase often attributed to management guru Peter Drucker (though there's no definitive proof he said those exact words). Mark Fields, Ford Motor Company's former CEO, popularized it, and word on the street is that the quote still hangs in Ford's war room today.

Who said it first doesn't really matter. The principle is solid. When culture and strategy clash, culture wins every time. Like a heavyweight champion, culture will pummel, kill, destroy, and override every strategic planning effort you've put in place, no matter how carefully crafted.

Too many organizations don't seem to get this. They treat culture as an afterthought when it should be the foundation of every business decision. You know the drill — toss out an employee engagement survey twice a year, have HR recite the company values during the annual town hall, and check the "culture box." Done and dusted.

Checking boxes, though, won't help you create a culture where people actually want to come to work, feel genuinely valued, and believe in the company's direction. Creating the kind of culture that supports your strategy AND the people who bring that strategy to life is about creating an environment where they can bring their full selves to work and do their best.

This isn't the soft, fuzzy stuff, people — it's the hard work that determines whether your strategy lives or dies. And in today's workplace, where the competition for talent is fierce, it's what separates the organizations that dominate from those that merely survive.

Whether you lead a team, aspire to move into leadership, or simply want to navigate your organization more effectively, understanding this culture-strategy connection matters deeply. If you're an individual contributor, recognizing how culture shapes decisions helps you position your ideas for success. If you're an emerging leader, building cultural awareness now prepares you to drive meaningful change later. And if you're already in a leadership position, mastering these principles might be the difference between your strategic vision becoming reality or yet another abandoned initiative.

The approaches I'll share in this chapter apply no matter where you sit in the organizational chart because culture is built and sustained through thousands of daily interactions at every level.

What is Company Culture?

The conference room felt thick with tension. I was sitting just close enough to overhear the conversation between the Head of Supply Chain and my direct manager. Their words hung in the air, casual yet loaded with implications that would reverberate far beyond this moment.

"She'll be a good fit for the manager position," the Head of Supply Chain said, "we need more diversity, and she's a woman of color."

In that instant, I knew exactly what was happening. This wasn't a genuine celebration of talent or potential. This was cultural performativity at its worst—reducing a qualified candidate to demographic checkmarks rather than recognizing her individual capabilities.

The irony wasn't lost on me. An attempt to demonstrate inclusivity was, in fact, doing the exact opposite. Worst of all, the candidate they were discussing, who did indeed become the new manager, knew exactly what was happening too. She would later confirm my suspicions by leaving the organization after just six months, feeling more like a token than a valued team member.

From a purely business perspective, this moment represented more than just a missed opportunity. It was a costly mistake. Consider the investment: hours of recruiting, interviewing, onboarding, and training, all dissolved in less than a year.

 **TRUTH BOMB**

According to a Gallup poll, replacing an employee can cost anywhere from 50% to 200% of their annual salary—a staggering expense for organizations of any size.[12]

If the financial costs aren't enough to convince you that culture matters, consider that the damage extends far beyond financial metrics. As a woman of color myself, I immediately began to question my own standing in the organization. Was I also seen as just a check in a box? Would every achievement be filtered through the lens of my demographic identity? Hearing my superiors talking about

---

12 Shane McFeely and Ben Wigert, "This Fixable Problem Costs U.S. Businesses $1 Trillion," *Gallup*, March 13, 2019 (https://www.gallup.com/workplace/247391/fixable-problem-costs-businesses-trillion.aspx#:~:text=The%20cost%20of%20replacing%20an,to%20%242.6%20million%20per%20year).

another employee as a token left me feeling undervalued. As a result, I found myself overcompensating, stressing about every interaction, believing that my mistakes would not just reflect poorly on me, but on every person who shared my identity markers.

If you've ever had a similar moment — that sinking realization that you might be seen as filling a quota rather than adding value — you know exactly what I'm talking about. You've felt that pit in your stomach when you wonder if your promotion was about your performance or your demographics. You know the exhausting mental gymnastics of second-guessing every interaction, every mistake, every success.

Working in an environment where employers treat inclusivity in particular and company culture in general as a box-checking exercise undermines trust, engagement, and productivity while damaging employee well-being.[13] When you're constantly wondering if you truly belong or if you're just there to make the company look good, it's impossible to bring your full self to work. The ripple effect of such a culture is profound and destructive, especially for those of us who already feel like we're on the outside looking in.

What I was witnessing was not genuine cultural evolution, but what Maren Gube, Cynthia Mathieu, and Debra Sabatini Hennelly call "carewashing," superficial gestures of care and inclusion that ultimately undermine the very values they claim to support.[14] And it creates an environment where employees feel more like commodities than contributors.

BRIDGING THE GAP: HR'S NEW COMMUNICATION MANDATE IN A MULTI-GENERATIONAL WORKPLACE

When we talk about company culture, our minds often turn to HR. HR professionals find themselves in a uniquely vulnerable position today, navigating the complexities of talent acquisition and retention through an intergenerational lens. As Baby Boomers

---

[13] Timothy R. Clark, "The Hazards of a 'Nice' Company Culture," *Harvard Business Review*, June 25, 2021 (https://hbr.org/2021/06/the-hazards-of-a-nice-company-culture).

[14] Maren Gube, Cynthia Mathieu, and Debra Sabatini Hennelly, "How 'Carewashing' Alienates Employees," *Harvard Business Review*, June 10, 2024 (https://hbr.org/2024/06/how-carewashing-alienates-employees).

have largely retired, Millennials now constitute the largest segment of the workforce, while Gen X employees hold the highest tenure positions. This demographic shift has created a significant social gap in workplace dynamics.[15]

The challenge of acquiring top talent has fundamentally changed. Today's entry-level candidates are asking themselves: "Is this work meaningful to me?" Many employees simply don't feel connected to their "why," the purpose that drives their commitment to an organization. HR professionals must acknowledge this vulnerability and address the widening gaps between GenXers and Millennials. To give just one example: while Millennials gravitate toward texting and DMs for communication, GenXers often prefer in-person interactions and email correspondence.

In this evolving landscape, communication has emerged as a critical superpower for HR professionals. Three focal points are particularly essential:

Emotional Intelligence: First, emotional intelligence has become more critical than ever before. Today's workforce is primarily seeking work that aligns with their core values rather than simply pursuing financial gain. HR leaders must understand these motivations to connect effectively with employees.

Emotional Regulation: Second, emotional regulation has transformed how we approach difficult conversations. What was once straightforward ("You've been coming in late. It's not a good look.") no longer represents a healthy way to deliver constructive criticism. Instead, the new approach emphasizes understanding, empathy, and care: "We've noticed a change. We want you to succeed. What support do you need from us?" Many resist this shift initially, perceiving any attempt to "soften" delivery of candid criticism as weakness, when in reality they've become organizational strengths.

---

15 Joe Waters, "Perspective | Young Americans Are Lost. Here's How to Help Them Find Their Way," *EdNC*, March 31, 2025 (https://www.ednc.org/perspective-young-americans-are-lost-heres-how-to-help-them-find-their-way).

Delegation: Finally, delegation has taken on new importance as teams combat burnout. From an HR perspective, two areas demand focus: effective delegation and the distinction between leading versus managing. Too many team leaders remain engrossed in day-to-day operations rather than embracing their roles as visionaries who can inspire and guide their teams toward meaningful objectives.

LET'S MAKE COMPANY CULTURE MORE THAN A BUZZWORD

There's no denying that the phrase "company culture" has become a buzzword. At least since the end of the Covid pandemic when many companies began bringing their workforce back into the office, there has been a mad dash for companies to prove that their office culture is healthy. However, in this mad dash, too many organizations have started treating "culture" as performative, offering perks like employee well-being days and yoga in the breakroom. Employees see right through these types of performative gestures, viewing them for what they are: little more than carewashing. There's nothing wrong with giving employees perks, but all the perks in the world can't make up for the problematic behavior, words, and attitudes of leaders.

Aligning culture and strategy requires much more nuance. Let's consider what company culture is.

Here's a definition: Company culture is the collection of shared values, beliefs, behaviors, and practices that shape how work gets done within an organization. It's essentially the personality and character of a company—the unwritten rules and expectations that influence how people interact, make decisions, and approach their work. Company culture is powerful because it operates largely through implicit understanding rather than explicit rules.

>  **TRUTH BOMB**
>
> Company culture is the living, breathing essence of an organization—the collection of shared values, beliefs, behaviors, and rules that shape how work gets done.

You can think of your organization's culture like an operating system. Just as a computer's OS determines how all programs function, your company's culture determines how everything else operates, including what leadership says and consistently does. It includes how decisions get made, how people get treated, and what behaviors get rewarded or ignored.

And here's why this matters: if you're someone who feels different, who brings a unique perspective, or who often finds yourself as the "only one in the room," you experience that operating system more intensely than anyone else. You feel every glitch, every inconsistency, every moment when the stated values don't match the lived reality.

One reason thinking of your company culture as a box-checking exercise won't work is because your company culture isn't a set of uniform behaviors or identical perspectives. A strong culture doesn't mean uniformity. The most effective organizations maintain core values while creating space for diverse perspectives and approaches. They understand that true inclusion isn't about making everyone the same, but about creating an environment where different approaches are not just tolerated, but actively valued.

This distinction matters deeply if you've ever felt pressure to minimize your differences or code-switch constantly, or if you wonder whether your success comes from your contributions or your demographics. When culture is genuine rather than performative, you can show up as your full self instead of expending precious mental energy trying to fit a mold that wasn't designed with you in mind.

The key is intentionality. Every organization needs to think deeply about what they mean by company culture. What policies, both written and unwritten, truly reflect your values? How will you know when those policies are working? And most importantly, how can you create a culture that doesn't just sound good on paper, but genuinely empowers and respects every individual?

Getting Real: Making Your Culture Support Your Strategy (Not Sabotage It)

Even the most thoughtful and well-crafted strategic initiatives cannot overcome a misaligned or toxic organizational culture.

So, as a leader or an aspiring leader, how do you ensure that your culture aligns with your strategy? You have to get real.

The following seven approaches have helped the organizations I've worked for and my clients:

1. Bottom-Up Beats Top-Down: Listen Before You Lead

Do you want to know the number one obstacle I bump up against when working with organizations trying to change their culture? Leaders thinking they can just hand down the goal and vision from on high.

Listen, you might get away with a top-down approach in certain situations, but when it comes to shifting company culture, a different approach is needed. People respond better when they feel included in the process rather than simply being told what to do. When employees feel like they're just being lectured instead of invited to contribute to solutions, engagement suffers and cultural initiatives struggle to gain traction.

Here's the deal: if you want high performance across your business, you absolutely must have real conversations with your people about what skills and values actually mean in practice. Not some HR checklist, but authentic dialogue. This is non-negotiable if you want effective change. And if you're concerned about the bottom line, here's what I know: when you operate according to values and goals, profitability follows.

Honestly ask yourself what would happen if you raised the following questions with your colleagues:

- **What does it mean to be on time?** Is on time showing up by 8:30 a.m. every day? Is on time showing up in time for your first meeting of the day? Is on time showing up at the time

that works best for you because most of your work can be done asynchronously?
- **What does employee engagement mean?** What are the signs that an employee in a particular position is engaged? Are they in their office eight hours a day and responding immediately to emails or DMs? Are they in the field interacting with customers? Are they bringing up concerns with their supervisors and colleagues?
- **What does it mean to complete assigned tasks?** Do you need to check in with your supervisor when you complete a task? Do you need to update the status in your task management system? Have your teams designed a workflow that everyone knows and follows?
- **What does success look like for deliverables?** What metrics are you using to measure success? Customer satisfaction? Repeat business? Positive customer reviews?

First, answer yourself. Then consider whether leaders, managers, and individual contributors would answer the same way? If the answer is "no," you've got work to do.

Trouble comes when leaders assume that everyone at the company translates their vision in the same way they do. Having conversations like this with everyone will reveal disconnects that might be sabotaging your strategy.

Don't mistake this exercise for a method to achieve uniformity across the board, though. Leadership must understand that cross-functional teams have unique perspectives and challenges. Getting genuine input requires a tailored approach that recognizes the diverse experiences of frontline employees across different departments. Communication needs look wildly different across teams. Your tech developers aren't processing information the same way your sales team does. That's just reality. So don't force everyone into the same communication box.

Make sure your policies have enough wiggle room to uphold your core values while letting each department breathe their own air.

When it comes to those annual reviews? Get creative! Build incentive structures that not only measure "did you hit your numbers" but also "did you actually live our values." This might mean creating custom metrics for different teams because what cultural contribution looks like for your customer service people isn't the same as what it means for your IT team. Different teams, different measures, same values. That's how you build something that sticks.

Additionally, if leaders do not genuinely embody the cultural values, morale will suffer. There's simply no way to "fake it until you make it" here. The goals, vision, and strategies promoted at the leadership level must all take into account the culture on the ground.

WHEN VALUES MEET THE TEST

When Sarah joined Northwestern Mutual as a mid-level manager, she was initially skeptical about the company's stated commitment to "leading with transparency and vulnerability." In her previous workplace, similar values were posted on walls but rarely practiced by leadership.

Three weeks into her role, Sarah was preparing her team for a major sales presentation when they discovered a critical error in their financial projections. The mistake would delay their proposal by at least a week, potentially jeopardizing the relationship with an important prospect.

Sarah begrudgingly scheduled a meeting with her VP, James, expecting to be reprimanded or told to push through with the flawed proposal to meet the deadline.

Instead, James listened carefully. He could sense Sarah's initial reluctance and her insecurities. The first thing he did was acknowledge her feelings and show her that he could relate. "Listen," he said, "I understand the stress and uncertainty here. I've been in your shoes." Then he shared a story about a time early in his career when he had made a significant pricing error on a major proposal. "About five years ago, I was leading a team pitching to our biggest prospect that year. The night before the presentation, my analyst found that we'd used the wrong growth projections in our calculations. The numbers looked great, but they were wrong. I was terrified to tell my boss, convinced I'd either be removed from the project or pressured to gloss over it. Instead of sleeping, I spent the night trying to fix it myself, making everything worse."

After validating Sarah's experience, putting her at ease, James asked, "What support do you need to make this right?" Rather than focusing on the missed deadline, he worked with Sarah to craft a message to the prospect explaining the situation. To Sarah's surprise, James insisted on joining the sales call.

On the call, James didn't throw Sarah's team under the bus or make excuses. He took accountability as a leader, explained the situation with complete transparency, and outlined their corrective plan. He concluded by saying, "We believe getting this right is more important than getting it done fast, and that's how we've built trust with our clients for over a century."

The prospect appreciated the honesty and ultimately signed a larger contract than originally discussed, specifically mentioning the transparency as a deciding factor.

Later, James shared this story at a company town hall, not to praise himself, but to reinforce how Northwestern Mutual's values translate into action. He highlighted how transparency builds stronger client relationships and creates internal psychological safety.

This story became part of the company narrative, repeated during onboarding and team meetings. It demonstrated Northwestern Mutual's commitment to transparency even when it was difficult.

Through this experience, Sarah understood that the company's culture wasn't just about what they said they valued, but how business got done. She went on to become one of the company's strongest cultural ambassadors, sharing this story with her own teams to demonstrate how strategy and culture aligned in practice.

2. Speak Their Language: Translating Strategy into Something People Actually Care About

Once your organization has established that leaders are listening to their people, it's important to check your strategy against that cultural context. To start, work with department heads to translate strategic objectives into meaningful narratives that connect with employees' values. Again, this is all about getting away from check boxes.

Emphasize that storytelling is key to communicating about the company culture. Just as your marketing team might use client or constituent stories to convey the impact of your work, we can all use storytelling to demonstrate how the strategy reflects the organizational identity and purpose.

For instance, suppose that your manufacturing company is guided by a "safety first" culture, and one of your frontline workers raises an issue with her manager. Not only would you want the manager to halt production and assemble a team to address the issue, but you would also want the employee to receive recognition for speaking up.

Feel free to get creative with such recognition. The form it takes is less important than connecting the dots between the value and the behavior. Perhaps the CEO could send the worker a personal email or sit down with her for a one-on-one conversation. Or you could recognize the employee more publicly, say, during the next company town hall. And to take this further, you could feature the story in future training materials as a way to illustrate that culture takes precedence over short-term production goals and to reinforce the point that employee voices truly matter.

> ## ⏱ TIME OUT
>
> I know this chapter has a lot of advice aimed at leaders. As an individual contributor, you may be wondering how it applies to you.
>
> First, this is essential background to help you evaluate the company culture in which you're swimming. Now you'll be able to recognize strong leadership when you see it, and just as importantly, spot the warning signs when you don't. This knowledge helps you make strategic decisions about where to invest your energy and whether your current organization can truly support your growth.
>
> Second, the seven approaches in this chapter can all be applied at any organizational level. You don't need a leadership title to influence culture around you. For example, you can translate your own goals and projects into language that resonates with what your leaders and colleagues actually care about. You can use storytelling to make your contributions more memorable and impactful. You can model transparency and vulnerability in your own interactions, creating the psychological safety that others crave.
>
> Third, understanding these principles positions you for future leadership opportunities. When you can articulate how culture and strategy connect, when you can spot dysfunction before it derails initiatives, and when you can communicate in ways that build rather than break down trust, you demonstrate leadership capability regardless of your current title.
>
> **Remember:** Some of the most influential people in organizations are those who understand how to create positive change through effective communication, starting exactly where they are.

Successful leaders know that culture is not like a microwave meal: "set it and forget it." It's more like a garden that you must tend to often to make sure it stays healthy and continues to support your company through any changes. Keep your culture on track by setting up two-way communication channels to gather input and address concerns.

3. Culture Roadblocks: Find Them Before They Wreck Your Strategy

Organizations that truly want to align strategy with culture will take deep dives into their culture on a regular basis. Instead of sending out an employee engagement survey once a year, and getting excited when you get a 5% return rate, conduct regular culture check-ins to identify misalignments between your current culture and strategic needs.

Employee engagement is a lot like going to the dentist. You sit in the chair and they praise you for having excellent oral hygiene. Your teeth are looking good! You wouldn't then go home and stop brushing your teeth because you had a good checkup. It's one thing to be happy about good results, but you wouldn't stop there. You would keep up the good work.

On the other hand, suppose you go to the dentist and they find some problems with your teeth. You have a few cavities or you need a root canal. You also wouldn't ignore your results in this case. You would make the appointment to have the work done as soon as possible and you would want to understand "how did I get here?" and "what can I do to make this better?"

The same is true for employee engagement. Most organizations survey their employees once or twice a year at the most. Think about that. Out of 365 days we spend maybe 7–14 of those (one to two weeks) assessing our culture. Let that marinate.

If you assess your culture and find that everything's great, good for you. Now what are you going to do to sustain that track record? And if you do find some roadblocks, don't procrastinate. The longer you wait, the harder it becomes to deal with the challenges.

As with everything in life, you will reap the harvest of the work you put in. Beyond employee engagement surveys, consider also using focus groups or one-on-one employee interviews to drill down into what folks are experiencing.

A comprehensive culture check-in should explore the following:

- Communication Patterns
- Leadership Behavior
- Workplace Dynamics
- Organizational Values in Practice
- Employee Experience Metrics
- Performance and Productivity Indicators
- Unwritten Rules and Norms
- Change Readiness

Ideally, these culture check-ins should be conducted quarterly with each department on a revolving basis. Culture check-ins should be conducted with leadership as well as with frontline employees.

In a perfect world, you would use an external team to conduct these assessments, cutting down on any internal bias that might cause you to overlook important challenges blocking strategy implementation and ensuring that employees feel free to speak their minds. After reviewing a cultural or employee engagement assessment, you'll gain insights into what's really happening on the ground.

This approach helped one of my clients, a power company division, recognize that during the pandemic their employees were feeling insecure because leadership wasn't communicating effectively about what was happening. Rather than creating perfectly polished, politically correct messages, leaders needed to be transparent and vulnerable — something many avoid for fear of appearing weak.

How did we shift the culture? We implemented weekly "Ask Me Anything" (AMA) sessions where leaders shared their own challenges and setbacks. I also coached leaders on what to say to help establish trust. Even if they couldn't directly answer a question, they knew how to answer in a way that was transparent and human: "I don't have the answers today, but I'm committed to getting those answers for you. I promise that whatever you need is at the forefront of my deliverables." Within just a month, this regular communication created a dramatic shift in engagement by reigniting hope and demonstrating real leadership during uncertain times.

Finally, look for "cultural debt," accumulated practices and beliefs that no longer serve the organization. Rather than saying, "well, this is the way we've always done it," ask, "is this process serving our current needs?" Then adjust as needed.

4. Behavior Shift, Not Just Mindset Shift: Creating Change That Sticks

Based on the culture check-ins, create a list of behaviors that need to change. By focusing on specific behaviors that need to shift, rather than abstract cultural concepts, you'll be in a better position to enact meaningful and measurable change.

For example, instead of broadly promoting "innovation," focus on encouraging team members to share unfinished ideas during meetings or allocate time for experimental projects. By considering what behavior you'd like to see, you can reverse engineer your way into the changes you want to make.

Organizations should also establish psychological safety so employees feel comfortable trying new approaches without fear of punishment for well-intentioned failures. This might involve celebrating "productive failures" that generate valuable insights or implementing no-blame listening sessions.

Finally, recognition and reward systems should be designed to reinforce behaviors that simultaneously advance both cultural values and strategic objectives. When a customer service representative goes beyond transactional interactions to build relationships that lead to expanded business opportunities, that behavior should be highlighted and rewarded as exemplifying both the cultural value of customer connection and the strategic goal of growth.

5. Hire for Culture Energizers: Building Your "Difference Dream Team"

When building a team that strengthens your culture-strategy alignment, hiring and promotion decisions become powerful cultural levers. Seek candidates who are not only a "cultural fit" but also bring diverse perspectives and experiences. In addition, hire those demonstrating alignment with your organization's fundamental values. This careful selection creates teams where differences become strengths rather than sources of conflict.

When evaluating potential leaders, look beyond technical capabilities to assess how effectively they can nurture and develop the cultural elements most critical to your strategy. Remember that you can always teach and develop technical skills, but it's much harder to train someone in cultural sensitivity or emotional intelligence.

The best cultural leaders create environments where others naturally engage in behaviors that drive strategic success. They are culture energizers. By treating cultural contribution as a non-negotiable qualification for advancement, you signal that culture-building is essential work that directly supports your organization's strategic ambitions.

6. Track What Matters: Measuring Culture Beyond the Fluffy Stuff

You can't manage what you don't measure. You can't hold people accountable to a metric they're not committed to delivering. If you want your culture to actually support your strategy, you've got to track more than just quarterly revenue and expenses. You need metrics that show whether your culture is doing what it's supposed to do — supporting your strategic priorities. If not, it is essential to go back into the lab and reassess not just what's getting done, but how it gets done. I'll dive deeper into specific metrics in Chapter 8.

One of my clients, the Wisconsin LGBT Chamber of Commerce, was dealing with a tricky situation as the political climate around LGBTQIA+ issues in the U.S. kept shifting. Despite making intentional changes to their strategic initiatives, they were seeing more employees walk out the door. When we dug into it, we discovered the real issue wasn't the strategy itself. It was that the underlying culture wasn't ready for the changes they were implementing around things like gender-inclusive restrooms and pronoun usage.

Here's what often happens: Organizations exhaust too much invaluable time and energy on things they can't solve, fix, or change. This takes away from where they can actually make a measurable, tangible impact. In this case, leaders at the Wisconsin LGBT Chamber of Commerce were so focused on pushing top-down culture change that they forgot to listen to their employees.

As a leader, it is crucial to accept the reality that not everyone is going to agree. Not everyone will want to comply. You have to accept that reality and be okay with them organically removing themselves from the organization. Otherwise, you're going to continue to see an increase in turnover with people who are disconnected from the mission as well as people who are connected but don't feel that you are investing in them with time, energy, and recognition.

Once you know what to measure, build cultural considerations directly into your strategic planning process. Start thinking of strategy and culture as evolving together. They aren't separate things. To begin building culture and strategy together, try adding a cultural development phase into your timeline before major implementation milestones, for example. When you treat culture as something that grows and changes alongside your strategy, rather than just a static background condition, you create an organization that can adapt to change while still keeping its core identity and purpose intact.

> ### TIME OUT
>
> Let's take a pause because right now I can hear your brain moving 1,000 miles per hour. This is valid. And one of the things I'm hearing your brain say is "oh no, I've done this before." Or "how can I get this done in this climate?"
>
> First, let me remind you that the human brain sometimes needs to be (re)directed toward putting our time and energy into what we can actually change and influence. This is one of those moments. I want to give you some time to take a breath, slow down, and think about where you can activate your unique capabilities (more on this in Chapter 3).

> If you're feeling overwhelmed, you're not alone. Let's reset. You got this! You're a great leader. Take a breath.
>
> Don't worry! I'll wait while you take a breath.
>
> Alright. Now that you've reset, let's get back into it.

7. Communication That Survives a Storm: Building Resilience into Your Message

Organizations that successfully navigate change build communication resilience into their cultural foundation. Think of it like weatherproofing your house before a storm hits. You don't wait until it's pouring to fix the roof! We know it's a whole lot easier to make repairs when the sun is shining. Yet too often, we wait until the storm is here before we get into repair mode with our communication.

Remember that you can rebuild, restructure, and restore while the sun is shining. I encourage you to do this not only for your own sanity, but also because we know, at some point, a storm will come.

Do you have communication systems that can withstand turbulence? Notice, these should be flexible frameworks that bend without losing their core shape, rather than rigid structures that break under pressure. Your values stay intact while your messaging adapts to whatever crazy situation you're facing.

At the same time, develop leaders who can communicate with realness when things get messy. I mean having a conversation that acknowledges, "Hey, this is tough, but here's where we're going and why I believe we'll get there." This is so much more effective than perfectly polished corporate messages that sound like they came from a robot (and probably did!).

For example, one of my clients was a manager struggling to connect with team members. As a self-proclaimed introvert and internal processor, this manager had difficulty speaking out during meetings. Because the company culture was such that speaking during meetings was how you "proved" you were engaged and a strong leader, this manager was perceived as being checked out.

Many ambitious go-getters automatically think being the loudest in the room equals being the most impactful. However, successful organizations understand that introverted, soft-spoken individuals aren't less engaged — they're processors! I call these individuals "quiet storms" and we talk about them more in Chapter 7.

The most successful organizations weave culture right into strategy execution. They don't treat culture like some separate HR project. They get that strategy is what you aim to do, while culture determines how you'll do it. When these elements align, your strategy implementation flows naturally.

The bottom line? Own your communication style, help others understand and anticipate it, and build systems that value different voices. That's true communication resilience.

Summary: 7 Approaches to Making Your Culture Support Your Strategy

Approach	Summary
1. Bottom-Up Beats Top-Down: Listen Before You Lead	Instead of dictating culture from above, create authentic dialogue about what skills and values mean in practice for different teams and departments.
2. Speak Their Language: Translating Strategy into Something People Actually Care About	Transform strategic objectives into meaningful narratives that connect with employees' values and use storytelling to demonstrate how the strategy reflects organizational identity.
3. Culture Roadblocks: Find Them Before They Wreck Your Strategy	Conduct regular culture check-ins to identify misalignments between current culture and strategic needs, using focus groups and interviews to uncover what's really happening.
4. Behavior Shift, Not Just Mindset Shift: Creating Change That Sticks	Focus on specific behaviors that need to change rather than abstract cultural concepts and establish psychological safety where people feel comfortable trying new approaches.
5. Hire for Culture Energizers: Building Your "Difference Dream Team"	Seek candidates who bring diverse perspectives while demonstrating alignment with fundamental values, treating cultural contribution as a non-negotiable qualification.

Approach	Summary
6. Track What Matters: Measuring Culture Beyond the Fluffy Stuff	Track metrics that show whether your culture is supporting strategic priorities by measuring not just what gets done, but how it gets done.
7. Communication That Survives a Storm: Building Resilience Into Your Message	Create flexible communication frameworks that maintain core messaging while adapting to changing circumstances and develop leaders who can communicate authentically during turbulence.

Communication as the Rocket Fuel for Cultural Transformation

You're an extraordinary leader, right? Well, extraordinary leaders require extraordinary resources to do their jobs. So, when you think about the fuel that standard automobiles use versus the type of fuel that rocket ships use, there's a profound difference in potential. Regular gasoline might get you across town, but it will never allow you to break through the atmosphere.

Average leaders see communication as standard fuel — something necessary just to keep the engine running. But extraordinary leaders? They recognize communication as rocket fuel — the high-octane substance that generates enough power to escape gravity's pull, overcome seemingly impossible barriers, and reach destinations others can't even imagine. When you transform your communication from merely functional to genuinely transformative, you're no longer just driving the company car. You're commanding a vessel capable of taking your entire organization to new frontiers.

We can talk about bridging the traditional gap between strategy and culture all day long, but what all of this really comes down to is communication. Effective cultural transformation requires treating communication not just as a skill but as a strategic imperative that drives organizational change from the inside out. When organizations view communication merely as a tool for information sharing, they miss its profound influence on how people experience, interpret, and shape the culture around them. So, can we stop calling communication a "soft skill," please?

This is where my expertise comes in. I know that communication patterns reveal what an organization truly values. The topics leaders prioritize in meetings, the questions they ask (or don't ask), and how they respond to challenges all send powerful signals about what behaviors are expected and rewarded. These signals create the invisible architecture of culture that guides daily decisions at every level.

 TRUTH BOMB

Communication is about creating understanding, building trust, and driving meaningful organizational transformation. These are the building blocks of a genuinely healthy corporate culture.

Organizations undergoing cultural transformation must audit both their formal and informal communication channels. Formal systems (e.g., town halls, email updates, performance reviews) should consistently reinforce desired cultural elements. Equally important, though, are the informal conversations happening throughout the organization that often have an even greater influence on behavior.

Leaders who successfully transform culture recognize that every interaction presents an opportunity to demonstrate what the evolving culture looks like in practice. When former CEO of Best Buy, Hubert Joly, first started in the role without any prior retail experience, he openly admitted his lack of expertise and sought help from employees across the organization, including frontline store associates. Whenever he met a new employee, he famously said, "My name is Hubert, and I need help."

This became a cornerstone of Best Buy's cultural transformation and eventual turnaround success. Because here's the thing: When a CEO asks his team members for help, using the explicit words "I need help," it creates a layer of autonomy and meritocracy, which the team member translates into "I belong here. I'm valued here. I can win here." This act of vulnerability not only demonstrated his willingness to learn, but also fostered trust and collaboration within the company.[16]

This example demonstrates that the most powerful cultural transformations occur when organizations create communication ecosystems where everyone can contribute to shaping the culture, rather than relegating some to merely interpreting it. This means building mechanisms for dialogue across hierarchical levels and encouraging the expression of diverse perspectives. When employees feel their voices genuinely matter in defining "how we do things here," cultural change becomes sustainable rather than superficial. Effective communication is crucial for creating the right culture that will support, rather than undermine, strategic initiatives.

By elevating communication from a supporting skill to a strategic driver of culture, organizations create the foundation for lasting transformation that aligns cultural strength with strategic ambition.

Remember that traditional saying we opened the chapter with: "Culture eats strategy for breakfast?" Well, with the approaches we've explored in this chapter, culture and strategy can finally sit down for a civilized meal together. In fact, they might even start swapping recipes instead of fighting over menu items. Because when you get communication right, culture and strategy bring out the best flavors in each other. And that's a breakfast worth waking up for.

---

16   Jan Koch, "How CEOs Define Vulnerability—and Benefit From It," *BCG*, June 18, 2024 (https://www.bcg.com/publications/2024/how-ceos-define-vulnerability).

The Real Talk Radar:
Your Communication Culture Check-Up

Let's cut to the chase: communication can make or break your organization's culture. Ready for some honest self-reflection? Rate each statement below on a scale that actually means something:

1 = Almost Never (We're talking unicorn-rare)
2 = Occasionally (Maybe when Mercury isn't retrograde)
3 = Sometimes (About as often as you clean behind the refrigerator)
4 = Often (Like your coffee habit)
5 = Almost Always (As reliable as gravity)

The Real Talk on Organizational Clarity

1. **Strategic Transparency:** Your leaders don't just share the "what" but the juicy "why" behind strategic decisions. Are they painting the full picture or just handing out puzzle pieces? (Rating: _____)

2. **Cross-Departmental Synergy:** Can your marketing team explain what engineering is up to? Does HR understand how sales targets affect their work? Or is everyone working in glorified silos? (Rating: _____)

3. **Information Democracy:** Does critical information flow freely across your organization, or does it get trapped like a VIP hostage in corner offices? (Rating: _____)

Leadership: Walking the Communication Walk

1. **Beyond Directives:** Leaders provide the context, backstory, and reasoning — not just marching orders. Are they treating employees like thinking partners or button-pushers? (Rating: _____)

2. **Truth-Telling Without Fear:** Employees have psychological runway to tell leaders the unvarnished truth without preparing their résumés afterward. (Rating: _____)

3. **Message Consistency:** Is your organization's story the same whether you're hearing it in the boardroom, breakroom, or Zoom room? (Rating: _____)

The Cultural Communication Vibe

1. **Psychological Bravery Zone:** Can team members voice the unspoken, challenge assumptions, or float "crazy ideas" without being subtly penalized or overtly shut down? (Rating: _____)

2. **Different Voices Amplified:** Your communication practices actively seek out and value perspectives from employees with different backgrounds, thinking styles, and communication preferences. (Rating: _____)

3. **Change Without Chaos:** During shifts and pivots, leadership communication is clear, empathetic, and frequent enough to prevent the rumor mill from becoming everyone's primary news source. (Rating: _____)

The Profit Zone: Where Communication Powers Performance

1. **Recognition Revolution:** Contributions are acknowledged, not with generic "great job" platitudes, but with specific recognition that makes people feel seen. (Rating: _____)

2. **Purpose Connection:** Beyond metrics and deadlines, communication illuminates how each person's work creates ripples of meaningful impact in the real world. (Rating: _____)

3. **Conflict as Catalyst:** Communication friction points aren't swept under the rug or allowed to build up — they're addressed directly, constructively, and with enough emotional intelligence to strengthen rather than strain relationships. (Rating: _____)

The Moment of Truth: Your Score

Total Score: _____ (Add up all ratings)

Maximum Possible Score: 60

WHAT YOUR SCORE REALLY MEANS

0-20: Communication Emergency

Your organization needs communication CPR — stat! You're experiencing critical breakdowns that are undoubtedly tanking performance, trust, and team morale. The good news? You've nowhere to go but up.

21-40: The Communication Mediocrity Zone

You've got communication vital signs, but you're not exactly thriving. There's substantial opportunity to transform from merely functional to genuinely effective communication practices.

41-50: Communication Competence with Room to Shine

You're doing solid work! Now it's time to refine and elevate specific areas to transform your good communication culture into a truly great one.

51-60: Communication Excellence (No, Really!)

Congratulations! Your organization demonstrates the kind of sophisticated, human-centered communication approach that drives exceptional performance, deep trust, and genuine engagement. Don't get complacent, though — excellence requires continual nurturing.

BEYOND THE SCORE: WHAT NOW?

1. Look at your lowest scores. What's the one small but mighty change that could create the biggest communication shift in that area within 30 days?

2. What communication strength could you double down on, transforming it from merely "strong" to truly distinctive, possibly even becoming part of your organizational identity?

3. If you could implement just one new communication practice that would send ripples of positive change throughout your entire organization, what would it be?

Remember: Communication is about creating shared meaning, building trust, and bringing your organization's purpose to life every single day.

Chapter 2

The Hidden Costs of Culture Misalignment

"Do not expect you from others."

– Anonymous

Let's get real about something I've witnessed firsthand while working with organizations from startups to Fortune 100 giants: culture misalignment is a silent profit killer.

Sure, we can nod along when someone mentions "dysfunction" (and yes, we'll dive into those red flags shortly). In the corporate world, though, nothing speaks louder than cold, hard costs. And make no mistake: cultural dysfunction comes with a massive price tag that rarely shows up as a line item on your P&L statement. I've already shared several jaw-dropping stats, but here's another one for all my data-lovers out there:

- 83% of those who rate their workplace culture as good or excellent are motivated to produce high-quality work. Compare that with the 45% of respondents who rated their company cultures as terrible or poor.[17]

We desperately need to uncover the hidden costs of culture misalignment.

---

[17] Tracy Lawrence, "Company Culture is Your Competitive Advantage — Unless You Ignore It," *Forbes*, February 3, 2025 (https://www.forbes.com/sites/tracylawrence/2025/02/03/company-culture-is-your-competitive-advantage-unless-you-ignore-it/).

Why Surface the Costs?

"Why do we need to surface the costs?" You might ask. Two reasons:

1. To light a fire under decision-makers who control the purse strings and resources needed for real change;
2. To create the collective "oh sh*t" moment about what's actually at stake if we, as leaders and as individuals, continue the corporate equivalent of ignoring the check engine light.

When organizational culture goes sideways, we're not just talking about uncomfortable meetings or awkward hallway interactions. What too many executives miss is how cultural toxicity is like the check engine light that keeps flashing while the strange noise under the hood gets louder. Everything might look fine on the dashboard (e.g., revenue numbers holding steady, projects completing on schedule), but the underlying systems are deteriorating. By the time the problems become unmistakable, the damage is often extensive and far more costly to repair than if addressed at the first warning signs.

I experienced this disconnect firsthand while working for a notable company supporting what appeared to be a high-performing business in manufacturing and warehousing. We saw senior leadership, trustees, and shareholders celebrating because we were crushing our targets. Those stakeholders were saying, "We're kicking butt. We're proud." The dashboard looked perfect.

But I'm always looking beyond dashboards to the people. Working directly with manufacturing employees and managers every day, I wasn't experiencing that same success story. I saw significant tension brewing behind what appeared to be a high-performing division. People were showing up to town halls and meetings, but they weren't speaking up. They believed their ideas would only be received well if they were shared with a positive tone, if they said what senior executives wanted to hear.

This was 2013, not that far removed from the 2008–2009 financial crisis. People were still cautious, much like today as we emerge from the Covid pandemic. I saw all these talented, hardworking employees working their butts off, but the changes being implemented were starting to disengage team members.

I told my manager at the time, "We've got a culture problem brewing. I know we don't see it yet in the numbers, but let me tell you what I'm seeing…"

 TIME OUT

How many times have you seen a metric dashboard that truly focuses on people and culture versus on-time shipments, order fulfillment, or other revenue-generating activities? I'm willing to bet you've rarely or never seen it because I have rarely seen it myself.

My manager, who had an engineering background and was very analytical, responded predictably: "Let's not stir up anything. We're hitting our numbers. Denise, I just need you to navigate this, work with these people. That's why you're here, that's why you're in this role." He was essentially saying, 'fix it behind the scenes, don't complicate our good numbers.'

That conversation put me in a position in which I realized we desperately needed metrics around team member morale and collaboration. As my daily devotional reminded me that morning: "Be quick to listen and slow to talk or get angry." When you learn to listen, even when everything seems fine on the surface, it's not just about the numbers anymore. It's about how people are feeling, especially when they're still expected to perform at high levels in an ambiguous, rapidly changing environment.

Sure enough, we started seeing people leave the company. That's when I learned that as leaders, we must lean into those red flags. When I brought this to my leader's attention, it came from a place of care, not a desire to stir up trouble. Leaders must listen to their trusted team members when they raise these concerns because if you ignore them, it's going to cost you far more in the end.

Dysfunction thrives in environments where:

- Communication has devolved into carefully crafted corporate theater.
- Transparency has been replaced by politically choreographed performances.
- Relationships have transformed from genuine connections into strategic alliances.

The result? A workplace where people bring their carefully curated professional masks instead of their full, brilliant selves. Where energy gets diverted to navigating politics rather than solving problems. Where innovation stalls because it's safer to nod along than speak truth.

Recognizing these patterns is your first critical step toward building a culture where honest communication creates the conditions for both human and financial thriving. Because let's face it: the organizations that figure this out are eating everyone else's lunch in the marketplace (Yep. In the last chapter, we were talking about breakfast. Now, we've moved on to lunch!).

Red Flags That Are Costing You (More Than You Think)

Did you know:

- 72% of U.S. employees who have experienced unfair treatment at work due to their weight say it has made them feel like quitting their jobs?[18]

---

18 Matt Gonzales, "Confronting Weight Bias and Discrimination in the Workplace," *SHRM*, January 6, 2024 (https://www.shrm.org/topics-tools/news/all-things-work/confronting-weight-bias).

- More than 40% of workers over 40 report experiencing age discrimination at work in the last three years?[19]
- Covering — the act of hiding aspects of one's identity — is something 61% of employees do at work, and the numbers are higher for minorities (83% of LGBTQ individuals, 79% of Black employees, and 63% of Latinx employees report covering at work)?[20]
- Over 40% of Asian American professionals feel pressured to conform to model minority stereotypes, avoiding behaviors that might be seen as "too assertive" or "too emotional?"[21]
- Many professionals of color avoid discussing their cultural background, family, or political perspectives at work due to fears it might hinder their career progression or cause discomfort among white colleagues?[22]
- The act of masking one's true identity — while often unconscious — can lead to chronic stress, anxiety, and burnout among employees of color?[23]
- Only 3% of Black professionals say they feel "completely comfortable" being their authentic selves at work?[24]
- Inclusion efforts that fail to address identity masking can unintentionally reinforce harmful norms and leave people of color feeling more isolated?[25]

---

19 Erica Pandey, "The American Workplace's Bias Against Age," *Axios*, September 2, 2023 (https://www.axios.com/2023/09/02/ageism-age-discrimination-statistics-america-2023-workplace).

20 "Uncovering Talent: A New Model of Inclusion," *Deloitte*, 2013 (https://www2.deloitte.com/content/dam/Deloitte/us/Documents/about-deloitte/us-about-deloitte-uncovering-talent-a-new-model-of-inclusion.pdf).

21 Neil G. Ruiz, Carolyne Im, and Ziyao Tian, "Asian Americans and the 'Model Minority' Stereotype," *Pew Research Foundation*, November 20, 2023 (https://www.pewresearch.org/race-and-ethnicity/2023/11/30/asian-americans-and-the-model-minority-stereotype/).

22 "Coequal Research Study Examines How Workplace Interactions Between Mangers and Colleagues Contribute to Inequities and Unfairness," *Coequal*, November 16, 2021 (https://coqual.org/wp-content/uploads/2021/11/Equity-2-press-release-1.pdf).

23 "Stress in America 2020: A National Mental Health Crisis," *American Psychological Association*, 2020 (https://www.apa.org/news/press/releases/stress/2020/report-october).

24 "Being Black in Corporate America: An Intersectional Exploration," *Coqual* (formerly Center for Talent Innovation), 2019 (https://coqual.org/reports/being-black-in-corporate-america-an-intersectional-exploration).

25 "Honoring Identity to Activate Equity," *Deloitte*, 2024 (https://www2.deloitte.com/content/dam/Deloitte/us/Documents/us-deloitte-self-id-journey-article-2024.pdf).

I know. Seeing statistics listed like this can be overwhelming. However, when we slow down and dig deeper, we see that it's a reality check about what's happening beneath the polished surface of our workplaces. If you haven't walked in these shoes or regularly engaged with these communities, there's a rich tapestry of lived experiences waiting for you to discover — perspectives that could transform how you lead and communicate. And look, no one's expecting you to single-handedly dismantle systemic inequities that have been baking for centuries. But keeping these realities front and center is all about having the context you need to make decisions that don't accidentally perpetuate the same old patterns.

 TRUTH BOMB

We must accept that "isms" are a problem that cannot be solved. "Isms" will never go away. However, we can focus on ways to change or influence how we navigate through these "isms."

Cultural dysfunction manifests through numerous indicators that become increasingly evident as problems take root. If you're tempted to brush off these warning signs — understandably to avoid conflict — the reality is that as a high performer, you're likely confronting systemic cultural breakdown.

Here are some of the symptoms you might notice as a leader or as an observant individual within the organization:

Revolving Door Syndrome: High turnover rates, particularly among specific demographic groups, signal serious culture problems. When an organization invests in recruiting diverse talent only to see them leave within months, the message is clear: the culture isn't truly inclusive. For example, a McKinsey study looking at women in the workplace notes that "women leaders are more than 1.5 times as likely" (compared to men at the same occupational level) to have left a previous job because of wanting to work for an employer that was more committed to inclusion and belonging.[26]

Disconnected Leadership: When executives make decisions in isolation from those responsible for implementing the changes, the resulting disconnect creates friction at every level. Goals cascade from leadership with little understanding of ground-level realities, creating policies that employees find impractical or even contradictory to stated values. This disconnect creates inefficiency and breeds cynicism.

Communication Chasms: In dysfunctional cultures, people struggle to articulate thoughts clearly, fail to actively listen, and hesitate to speak up. Meetings become exercises in talking past one another or enduring awkward silences, and projects suffer from constant misunderstandings and rework. These communication failures compound over time, creating project delays that directly impact revenue.

Post-Pandemic Withdrawal: The increasing tendency toward social isolation (e.g., employees reluctant to engage in face-to-face interaction, becoming more introverted, and avoiding collaborative settings) severely impacts innovation. Even senior leaders express this sentiment behind closed doors, though rarely publicly. This withdrawal doesn't just affect relationships; it fundamentally undermines the collaborative foundation necessary for complex problem-solving.

The Leadership Tightrope: Leaders find themselves unable to effectively motivate high performance without sounding authoritative or feeling like a dictator. They walk a precarious thin line between demonstrating empathy and awkwardness, creating inconsistent management approaches that confuse and frustrate teams. The result? Disengagement and reduced discretionary effort.

---

26 "Women in the Workplace," *McKinsey*, 2022 (https://www.mckinsey.com/~/media/mckinsey/featured%20insights/diversity%20and%20inclusion/women%20in%20the%20workplace%202022/women-in-the-workplace-2022.pdf).

"Othered" Experiences: When employees feel marginalized (whether they're single workers without children who receive disproportionate workloads, introverts in extroverted environments, or members of underrepresented groups) they withdraw their full participation. Their valuable perspectives remain unshared, and their talents underutilized.

Simmering Resentment: Tensions between demographics, generations, and work styles create undercurrents of conflict that divert attention from productive work. These tensions rarely explode dramatically. They simply drain energy slowly day after day, like a leaky faucet, creating a persistent drag on performance and well-being.

Boundary Confusion: In evolving workplace cultures, leaders report struggling with the many boundaries that people now have, making real connection challenging. It's true that we're seeing intergenerational trends here. This uncertainty creates hesitation in communication, reduces psychological safety, and ultimately limits the development of trust necessary for high-functioning teams.

What's the Damage? Beyond the Balance Sheet

It's not hard to imagine that any of these challenges would negatively impact efficiency, effectiveness, and productivity throughout an organization. If you're experiencing any of the above, focusing on the specifics could change the game.

Unless you are really connecting the dots though, you might overlook the financial impact of these warning signs. I call these "Culture Tariffs":

- Productivity losses from miscommunication and rework average 20–25% of employee time in affected organizations. This challenge is well-documented in the construction industry, for example.[27]

---

[27] "Survey Estimates Time and Money Lost to Rework and Miscommunication," *The Construction Specifier*, August 8, 2018 (https://www.constructionspecifier.com/survey-estimates-time-and-money-lost-to-rework-and-miscommunication/).

- Companies with bad reputations typically need to offer at least 10% higher salaries to persuade candidates to accept job offers compared to companies with strong employer brands.[28]
- Organizations with inclusive cultures are 6 times more likely to be innovative and agile.[29]
- On average, employees reporting workplace stress miss 18 workdays per year due to stress-related challenges.[30]
- Navigating dysfunction often means more meetings, second-guessing, and political maneuvering, which slows down decision-making and increases the likelihood of errors or missed opportunities.[31]
- Disengaged employees are less likely to provide exceptional service, leading to more customer complaints and a decline in overall customer experience.[32]

Perhaps most significantly, dysfunctional cultures make organizations vulnerable to disruption. As one executive observed, "When our culture was struggling, we couldn't execute even the most brilliantly conceived strategy — we were simply too busy managing internal friction to respond to market changes." This is a huge liability!

In the following sections, we'll explore how to address these dysfunctions through practical communication approaches that create cultures where people can bring their best selves to work and deliver their best results.

---

28 Wade Burgess, "A Bad Reputation Costs a Company at Least 10% More Per Hire," *Harvard Business Review*, March 29, 2016 (https://hbr.org/2016/03/a-bad-reputation-costs-company-at-least-10-more-per-hire).

29 Juliet Bourke and Bernadette Dillon, "The Diversity and Inclusion Revolution," *Deloitte Review*, January 2018 (https://www2.deloitte.com/content/dam/insights/us/articles/4209_Diversity-and-inclusion-revolution/DI_Diversity-and-inclusion-revolution.pdf).

30 Marsha Fisher, "Workplace Stress and Absenteeism Among Key Findings in Workplace Options Well-being Survey," *Workplace Options* (https://www.workplaceoptions.com/news/workplace-stress-and-absenteeism-among-key-findings-in-workplace-options-well-being-study/).

31 Edwin Eve, "The Impact of Dysfunctional Teams on Organisational Performance," *Eve Coaching and Consulting* (https://www.evecoachingconsulting.com/insights/impact-of-dysfunctional-teams-on-organisational-performance).

32 Noel Diem, "The Cost of Disengagement in the Workplace is High," *Mitratech*, December 1, 2023 (https://mitratech.com/resource-hub/blog/the-cost-of-disengagement-in-the-workplace-is-high/).

Communication and Cultural Transformation

If you notice any of these hidden costs and decide to work on cultural dysfunction in your organization, the best place to start is with communication. Transforming a dysfunctional culture happens through thousands of daily interactions in which effective communication builds trust, alignment, and shared purpose. Townhall meetings, grand pronouncements, and policy changes are traditional ways of transforming culture. In the current state and beyond, when leaders and team members master communication fundamentals, they create the foundation for lasting cultural change.

THE FUNDAMENTALS OF CONNECTION

1. Connecting to the Audience (and not just when you're on stage)

The most powerful communication begins with understanding who you're speaking to—not just their job titles, but their concerns, values, and perspectives. In organizations experiencing cultural dysfunction, people stop seeing each other as individuals and instead view colleagues through the lens of stereotypes, departments, or hierarchical positions (e.g., "she's one of those 'suits', so she only cares about what's on the spreadsheet").

Effective connectors do something different. They approach each interaction with curiosity about the person behind the title. They adjust their message based on what matters to the listener, not just what matters to them. This simple shift, focusing outward rather than inward, immediately strengthens relationships.

A senior executive I worked with struggled to understand why her strategic initiatives gained little traction despite her clear articulation. A mentor in business school had taught her to focus on the business case whenever she presented a strategic initiative. And that advice wasn't wrong! The problem came in the delivery. When we observed her communication style, the issue became evident: she spoke exclusively in financial terms to a team motivated primarily by innovation and impact. By reshaping her message to address what energized her audience, while maintaining the same strategic direction, she transformed resistance into enthusiasm.

Of course, this strategy can only work if you know your audience. What do you do when you need to connect with an unknown audience, like when you're on stage or working with a new team? Here we can take a page from the godfather of psychoanalysis, Sigmund Freud. Freud gave us invaluable insights into the brain's inner workings, and here's what you need to know: no matter how much you study communication styles or learning preferences, you'll never fully anticipate every individual in your audience.

The one common denominator? Every person sitting before you has a brain, and that brain processes information through four distinct channels. Whether we're making decisions or absorbing new concepts, we cycle through the following processing centers:

- Instinctive responses (our gut reactions)
- Emotional processing (how we feel about it)
- Reflective consideration (what it means to us personally)
- Rational analysis (logical evaluation of facts and consequences)

The most effective communicators are open to multiple approaches, deliberately crafting messages that touch all four processing centers. By hitting these neural pathways simultaneously, your message doesn't just land. It sticks, resonates, and ultimately drives action across diverse audiences.

2. Getting to the Point

In a world where attention is our scarcest resource, brevity is essential for impact. "Time is our greatest commodity," I often tell clients. Leading with your main idea, then adding supporting details only as needed and based on what your audience needs from you, fundamentally changes how your message is received.

This approach requires discipline and clarity of thought. It means ruthlessly prioritizing what others need to know versus what you'd like to say. When you respect others' time by being concise, you signal that you value them. This simple act builds goodwill that carries forward into future interactions.

Consider this contrast: a mid-level manager rambles on for 15 minutes giving context before stating what action is needed, while his colleague opens with "I need your approval on three key changes to the Murray project by Thursday. Here's why…" The second approach immediately engages the listener and focuses the conversation where it matters most.

3. Always Be the Same

Consistency in communication builds trust. When people experience you as real — the same person regardless of whether you're speaking with the CEO or an intern — they sense integrity. This doesn't mean being rigid or unchanging; it means that your core values and approach remain recognizable across contexts.

In organizations struggling with cultural dysfunction, people often adopt different personas depending on who they're talking to. This inconsistency creates distrust and confusion. When leaders demonstrate consistent communication across all interactions, they provide a model of humanness that others can follow.

> **TIME OUT**
>
> Okay, let's pause. I can hear your brain going 1,000 miles per hour again. Where are all my code-switchers at?
>
> The following is for all the code-switchers and people who are curious about code-switching because what I hear many saying is, "Wait a minute, DT. Always be the same? What about code-switching?" Let's get into it.
>
> While consistency builds trust, I want to acknowledge that many professionals, particularly those from underrepresented groups, have developed code-switching as a necessary skill for navigating workplace environments.

> This ability to adapt language, tone, or expression across contexts can be a survival strategy rather than evidence of a lack of humanness. By recommending that you always be the same, I'm not suggesting that we eliminate all adaptation, but rather create workplaces where everyone can bring more of their genuine selves to every interaction.
>
> True communication excellence means recognizing when adaptation serves connection versus when it depletes our sense of self. The ideal is not rigidity, but rather conscious choice in how we express our authentic core.

4. Share Relative and Relatable Challenges

Nothing builds connection faster than addressing the real challenges people face right now. Generic communication feels irrelevant; specific communication that acknowledges current realities feels like understanding.

Today's workplace struggles with unique communication challenges: post-pandemic social isolation, navigating inclusion across multiple dimensions of diversity, integrating technology with human connection, and finding the right balance between empathy and accountability. One way to improve workplace culture is to name these challenges directly. When you do so, people immediately recognize that you understand their reality.

A team leader I worked with transformed her relationship with her remote team during the pandemic, not by pretending everything was fine, but by acknowledging, "I know we're all experiencing screen fatigue and missing the energy of in-person collaboration. Can we talk about how we can make our virtual interactions more meaningful while respecting everyone's need for boundaries?"

TALK IS NOT CHEAP: HOW YOUR COMMUNICATION DRIVES REAL-WORLD RESULTS

The fundamentals of connection affect individual day-to-day interactions as well as longer-term goals. When leaders and teams make an effort to communicate with intention, they can work better together to navigate complex workplace scenarios.

Change initiatives succeed or fail based not on the quality of the plan (though that matters too, of course), but on how effectively the case for change is communicated across different stakeholder groups. Leaders who can translate organizational imperatives into personally meaningful benefits for team members create momentum instead of resistance.

Conflict resolution depends on the ability to truly hear others' perspectives without immediately formulating rebuttals. The fundamentals of active listening (e.g., reflecting back what you've heard, asking clarifying questions, and acknowledging emotions) transform potentially divisive disagreements into opportunities for deeper understanding.

Cross-functional collaboration thrives when participants can translate between the specialized languages of different departments, finding common ground in shared objectives rather than getting lost in terminology differences.

Innovation processes depend on creating environments where different perspectives are not just tolerated but actively valued. Communication that invites contribution from different viewpoints, especially from those typically "othered" in the organization, unlocks creative potential that homogeneous thinking cannot match.

Decision-making improves dramatically when leaders can clearly articulate the reasoning behind choices, especially unpopular ones. Transparency about constraints, considerations, and trade-offs builds trust even when the outcome isn't what everyone wanted.

>  **TRUTH BOMB**
>
> When an organization masters these communication fundamentals, cultural transformation follows naturally. People feel heard, valued, and connected to purpose. Silos break down. Inclusion becomes lived experience rather than policy. Trust replaces suspicion. And the organization develops the resilience to navigate change without fragmenting.

Communication becomes the catalyst for cultural transformation through the consistent practice of connecting with others in ways that acknowledge their reality and invite their best contributions.

The Foundation of Cultural Excellence

Communication skills represent far more than the ability to deliver compelling presentations or facilitate effective meetings. They form the bedrock upon which strong company cultures are built and sustained. Every organizational interaction—from casual hallway conversations to formal strategic planning sessions, from onboarding experiences to exit interviews—is shaped by the quality of communication flowing between participants. When leaders and team members alike develop the ability to listen deeply, speak authentically, and connect meaningfully, they create environments where trust flourishes, innovation accelerates, and people bring their best selves to work.

The organization that invests in communication as a core competency fundamentally transforms its cultural DNA, building resilience against market disruption and creating the conditions in which both people and profits can thrive simultaneously. In the end, the strongest company cultures emerge from the thousands of daily interactions where people feel truly seen, heard, and valued through authentic communication.

PART 2
OWN YOUR DIFFERENCE

We've spent Part 1 unpacking how communication shapes organizational culture, and because your success is your company's success, it's now time to get personal. What about YOU? How do you find and amplify your authentic voice when you're navigating workplaces that weren't designed with you in mind?

This question is the beating heart behind the title, *The Only One in the Room*.

Look, it's fantastic if organizations take my advice, invest in communication as a core competency, and create cultures where diverse voices thrive. AND we need to acknowledge the reality: organizational change moves at a glacial pace. Meanwhile, you're in the trenches, feeling the daily pressure to shape-shift, conform, or water yourself down just to get a seat at the table. We're here to change this. You need to discover YOUR value being "the only one in the room," so you can use your voice to communicate your worth.

The next two chapters are for anyone who's ever walked into a meeting and immediately thought, "I don't belong here." According to one survey, 20% of U.S. workers (1 in 5) strongly or somewhat disagree with the statement, "When I'm at work, I feel like I belong."[33]

Maybe it's your background, your communication style, your thought process, or simply that you bring perspectives that make the dominant group uncomfortable. If you've ever swallowed your words because they didn't fit the established narrative, these chapters are your playbook.

---

33 "2023 Work in America Survey," *American Psychological Association* (https://www.apa.org/pubs/reports/work-in-america/2023-workplace-health-well-being).

In Chapter 3, "Are You Fitting In or Belonging?," we'll dive into what I call the UVC Method, identifying the Unique Values and Capabilities that form your distinctive professional fingerprint. We're skipping the fluffy self-help exercises. What I share is a strategic framework for navigating the razor's edge between belonging enough to have influence and staying authentic enough to make a difference.

The magic happens when you transform what feels like "otherness" into your superpower. This means strategically positioning your differences as valuable organizational assets.

We also need to address the elephant in the room: generative AI. What does the introduction of AI-powered tools in the workplace mean for communication, for you, and for your career? In an AI-dominated future, technical skills alone won't save your career. Just as I said in the Introduction, performance is just the entry ticket. It won't take you to the next level. The same principles about learning the fundamentals of communication apply here. Treating communication as currency will help you stand out as the human you are.

Chapter 4 shows you how to develop a communication approach that makes you irreplaceable. We'll explore why the bland, corporate-speak version of you is actually the most vulnerable to becoming obsolete.

Along the way, you'll gain practical tools for elevating your personal brand through voice, perspective, and presence, ensuring that your unique viewpoint is actively sought after. Because when you communicate with distinction, you become the person others can't stop quoting in your absence.

 **TRUTH BOMB**

True leadership has nothing to do with your title and everything to do with your transformation. When you understand your distinctive value and communicate it effectively, you create a gravitational pull that transcends organizational charts. This is what I mean when I talk about owning your difference.

Whether you're just starting out, stuck in middle management, or sitting in the C-suite, these chapters offer a roadmap for finding and amplifying your voice in ways that advance both your career and your organization's success.

By the end of Part 2, you'll know exactly how to show up as your full, brilliant self while creating the kind of impact that makes people wonder how they ever functioned without your perspective. This is leadership in its purest form.

Chapter 3

Are you Fitting In or Belonging?

> "The people who matter don't mind
> and the people who mind don't matter."
>
> –Dr. Seuss

Every professional has faced that moment: standing on the threshold of a meeting room, about to step into a culture that doesn't naturally align with who you are. The air feels different. The language sounds foreign. The unwritten rules remain mysterious. And the question haunts you: Do I belong here?

This is especially true when you're the "only one in the room": the only woman, the only person of color, the oldest person, the youngest person, the only one without a prestigious degree, or the only one brave enough to share a different perspective from everyone else.

This tension between fitting in and belonging is exhausting. The constant self-monitoring, code-switching, and second-guessing drains the energy you could otherwise direct toward your actual work. If you've felt this way, dear reader, you have experienced the Adaptation Tax. Yet what choice do you really have? The alternative — being completely out of step with your organization's culture — can limit your impact and advancement opportunities.

Well, I'm here to teach you that you do have a choice. You don't have to sacrifice your humanness for belonging or vice versa. You can fit in without losing yourself!

>  **TRUTH BOMB**
>
> Fitting in is when your primary awareness is making others feel comfortable about your identity. Belonging is when others recognize your identity. This framing lifts the Adaptation Tax.

The strongest contributors in any organization aren't those who completely conform or those who rebelliously reject the culture. They're the individuals who understand both themselves and their environment well enough to navigate the middle path: bringing their unique contributions forward in ways that resonate within their cultural context.

As an individual contributor, I want you to ask yourself: "Am I fitting in or belonging?" As a people leader, I want you to ask yourself: "Am I leading a culture of fitting in or belonging?" It's exhausting to fit in, but it's liberating to belong.

This chapter will show you how to walk that path with confidence, starting with showing you how to operate according to your Unique Values and Capabilities (UVC).

Get Curious About Your Signature Strengths

When I work with clients facing the belonging-versus-fitting-in dilemma, we begin with a foundational truth: You cannot effectively navigate any environment until you know precisely what you bring to it.

It took me years to realize this. Throughout my career, I have always felt more like "the only one in the room" than not, which was to be expected working for Fortune 100 companies where I was always surrounded by people who were used to being the smartest in the room. On the outside — and I hope those in senior leadership or executive roles understand this — I was smiling. For a lot of us, we smile, we do what we're told. The conditioning is: don't challenge.

But I think there was an aha moment when I realized:

If I want to be regarded as a leader...

If I want to be regarded as a critical thinker...

If I want to be regarded as someone who influences and inspires...

Then I have to show up in these rooms even when I feel like I'm the only one. I have to show up in these rooms in a way that's going to change that. Now, not everybody is going to accept this, but at least I know I'm being true to myself. I still show up smiling. It's just that my smile is no longer a mask.

I am at a point now where I refuse to apologize for who I am. I don't apologize for my perspectives, and I definitely don't apologize for my UVC — my unique value of being able to connect and communicate effectively. I am someone who can naturally lead with empathy as well as conviction.

Once I had that aha moment, that's when I started speaking up. For some leaders and some people, I was "really loud" or "really this" or "really that," but when I stayed true to myself, I started seeing changes. I was getting invited to meetings I wasn't invited to before. I was speaking on stages that I never thought I would speak on. This eventually led to me traveling all over the world, speaking to people in Japan and South Africa.

When I started coaching others, I really wanted to help them know that they could do the same wherever they were in their career trajectory, whether they're entry level, mid to senior level, all the way up to executives. I wanted people to recognize their values. It's not about what everybody else is doing. You're unique. That's why the operative word is unique. When you fully embrace that gift (and that gift means, "what can I do organically that a lot of people struggle with?") you lean into your unique values and capabilities (UVC) as a strength.

As soon as you understand that your voice, in addition to your performance, should be your own, it is brilliant. You know who you are, and you start shining. You stop diminishing your light, you stop shrinking, and you really start shining through embracing those UVCs.

The Unique Values and Capabilities (UVC) method discussed in this chapter provides a structured approach to defining your distinctive contribution. Unlike generic strengths assessments or personality tests, the UVC method focuses specifically on the intersection between what matters deeply to you and what you do uniquely well.

Exercise: Are You Living Your UVC?

Before we dive into the method itself, let's determine whether you're currently aligned with your Unique Values and Capabilities (UVC) or operating outside it. Remember, your career stage doesn't matter. In fact, I'd recommend you revisit these questions quarterly or every six months throughout your career.

Grab your journal and answer these questions honestly:

1. **Work Energy Check:** At the end of most workdays, do you feel:

    - Energized and satisfied, even if tired?
    - Mentally and emotionally drained beyond normal fatigue?
    - Indifferent, neither particularly fulfilled nor depleted?

2. **Know Your Value:** Can you immediately name the three most valuable and distinctive contributions you make to your team? Not generic skills everyone in your role should have, but the specific capabilities that make your approach different?

3. **Decision Filter:** When faced with choices about how to approach your work, do you have clear internal criteria that guide those decisions, or do you primarily look to others' expectations?

4. **What Others Notice:** What patterns emerge in the positive recognition you receive? Do people consistently acknowledge certain qualities or contributions that align with what you believe about yourself?

5. **Performance Consistency:** In which situations does your performance noticeably drop? Are there particular types of tasks, environments, or interactions for which you struggle to maintain your usual standards?

6. **Voice Recognition:** How often do you find yourself thinking, "That's not really me" when reflecting on your workplace

behavior or communication? Write down any examples that come to mind.

7. **Value Conflicts:** Have you experienced situations in the past six months in which you felt pressured to act in ways that conflicted with your core values? Write down any examples that come to mind.

8. **Engagement Indicators:** Which aspects of your work consistently engage you most deeply? Which do you find yourself avoiding or procrastinating repeatedly?

If your answers reveal significant misalignment (e.g., energy depletion, unclear contribution, lack of internal decision criteria, inconsistent performance, frequent inauthenticity, value conflicts, or disengagement patterns), you're likely operating outside your UVC.

Don't panic! This misalignment doesn't mean you're in the wrong role or at the wrong organization. It simply indicates that you haven't yet fully identified or activated your unique contribution within your current context. The remainder of this chapter will help you address that gap.

The next question to ask yourself is Where can I adapt? Adaptability (without paying the Adaptability Tax) is about looking at each of your answers and thinking about where you can make some changes. It's also about shifting the focus from questions like How many hours did I work this week? to What was my impact?

Let me share what happened when I asked one of my coaching clients to answer these questions. Marcus was a finance executive who felt increasingly disconnected from his work. Despite his technical expertise and consistent promotions, he felt like he was "just going through the motions" and wondered if he needed to change careers entirely. He questioned whether he belonged.

Through the UVC process, Marcus discovered that while his analytical capabilities were strong, his truly distinctive contribution came from translating complex financial concepts into actionable insights for his non-financial colleagues. His deepest values centered on building understanding across different perspectives. Yet his current role had him focused almost exclusively on technical analysis with minimal cross-functional interaction.

Rather than abandoning his career or leaving his organization, Marcus worked with his leader to reshape his role. This is a great example of adaptability! He maintained his technical responsibilities while creating regular opportunities to serve as a financial translator for other departments. This adjustment brought his work into alignment with his UVC, dramatically increasing both his engagement and his impact. Plus, it set him up for success in future roles because now Marcus better understood and could communicate his unique contribution.

In the next section, I'll share the structured process for identifying your own UVC, providing you with the foundation needed to navigate any professional culture without compromising who you are at your core.

The UVC Method: Uncovering Your Superpower

I'm going to show you the process for identifying your Unique Values and Capabilities (UVC). It's critical to keep in mind that this is a process of uncovering. Identifying your UVC is not about discovering or seeking something outside of yourself. We're uncovering what's already there (just like Dorothy in the *Wizard of Oz*). It's about uncovering the distinctive intersection between your deepest values and your most natural capabilities. This is the space where you make contributions that others can't easily replicate.

Unlike generic career assessments, the UVC method doesn't place you in predetermined categories. Instead, it's a four- to five-week process I take my clients through that helps you articulate what makes your contribution singular (If you're curious about this process, please hop over to my website: realcommcoach.com.).

Here's a preview of the four-step process that will reveal your UVC with clarity and precision.

STEP 1: OWNING YOUR CORE VALUES

You may have done core value exercises in the past. How did it go? Do you refer to your core values on a regular basis? Do you even remember what you came up with? If not, it's probably because you were thinking about your values in a purely intellectual (or "box checking") way.

I want you to start thinking of your values in a different way, as the principles that drive your decisions when no one is watching. Here's an uncomfortable truth: between the ages of zero and 18 years old, you are conditioned by your peers, your parents, your teachers, television, and in today's world, social media. This means you adopt others' values probably without even realizing it. These early years are when your thinking is formed and influenced by others.

Then when you hit the adult mark (18, 19, or 21+), you start to question, learn, and unlearn things. This is the process of uncovering your own identity. But this process is challenging when you don't have the tools to support your independence.

Like you, I experienced this conditioning firsthand. Growing up in Evansville, a small town in Southern IN, I was taught to believe that in order to experience anything of high quality, I had to be in rooms that were predominantly white. As a Black woman, I absorbed certain messages from society that were reinforced by the images I saw. When I was a kid, I thought all white people were rich because that was the image I saw on shows like *Different Strokes*, *Silver Spoons*, and *Bensen*! I believed I needed to adopt the power of privilege based on how white families were depicted on these sitcoms. For example, sounding "white," acting "white," wearing my hair straight instead of natural, changing my tone, avoiding certain references, essentially erasing anything that was distinctive about my culture.

This is why television shows like *The Cosby Show, A Different World,* and *The Mary Tyler Moore Show* were so impactful for me. Watching these shows, I was exposed to a counter-narrative to what I was conditioned to believe in my younger years. These shows helped me begin to question those assumptions. They helped me see that there were rooms that looked different from the rooms I had grown used to.

That's why this first step is so critical. When I ask you to own your values, either you're introducing yourself to your new identity, or, as I like to say when I talk about this from the stage, you "allow me to reintroduce" you to your true self. Not just intellectually knowing your values, but owning your values helps you get there because it reveals your true purpose and principles.

Exercise: Identity Value Circle

To identify your true values (not what you think they should be), complete this identity value circle exercise:

Set a timer for 10-15 minutes and complete these sentences:

- I am... (roles, identities you claim)
- I believe... (your core beliefs about the world)
- I am learning... (areas of growth)
- I enjoy... (what brings you fulfillment)

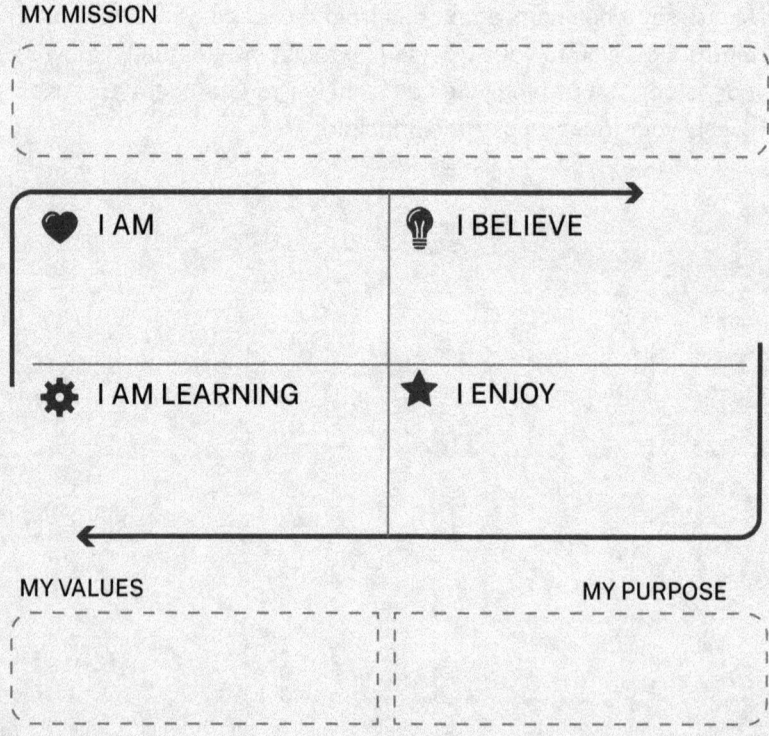

In the spirit of transparency, here's my identity value circle:

- I AM healthy and strong.
- I AM one of the greatest public speakers.
- I AM more than a conqueror.
- I BELIEVE there is more good in this world than evil.
- I BELIEVE what you put in is what you will get back.
- I BELIEVE that I can do all things through Christ, who strengthens me.
- I AM LEARNING to love me just the way I am.
- I AM LEARNING to be patient with the process.
- I AM LEARNING to forgive.
- I ENJOY eating good food.
- I ENJOY being around people who love life and love to laugh out loud.
- I ENJOY being at home alone.

As you review your identity value circle, look for patterns that reveal what truly matters to you. Pull out your journal again and consider:

Your Bold Moves: Think about three decisions you've made that others might have made differently. What underlying principles guided those choices? For example, did you choose a role with less prestige but more autonomy? Did you speak up when staying silent would have been easier?

Energy Tracking: For two weeks, note when you feel most energized and most depleted during your workday. Look beyond task difficulty to the nature of the work. Are you energized by collaborative problem-solving but drained by solo analysis? Energized by creating structure but drained by open-ended innovation?

What Drives You Crazy: Consider what consistently frustrates or angers you at work. These strong reactions often signal violated values. If you feel irritated when decisions are made without sufficient discussion, you likely value inclusive processes. If you feel frustrated when plans change frequently, you may value consistency and follow-through.

Your Legacy Statement: Imagine a colleague describing your impact five years after you've left the organization. What would you hope they'd say? Not about your technical accomplishments, but about how you approached your work and treated others?

After completing these reflections, identify patterns and distill them into 3–5 core values. Express your core values as short phrases like "intellectual integrity," "practical innovation," or "dignified inclusion." This will make them more memorable and provide more professional guidance. Notice that these may not be what you were expecting when I first mentioned owning your core values. They're different from the typical single-word values like courage, compassion, or accountability you may have chosen from a pre-determined list in the past.

 TIME OUT

Whoa! That was a lot! I know. Remember, I do each of these steps with my clients over the course of a whole week. If it feels good to take time between the exercises, give yourself the space you need.

There's no reason to rush this process.

If you feel overwhelmed, you can start with this simpler question:

If there were no resource constraints, budget constraints, or time constraints, what type of solutions would you offer based on your current role?

We often avoid dreaming in this way because we create, design, and invent from the mindset of restrictions. When I was at GE, for example, I was the leader of an African American employee resource group. The one big challenge we had was the budget. As a group, we had audacious goals that we brought to the attention of the executive team.

> I'll never forget the question one leader asked us: "What would you do if you had no constraints?" It was so liberating to have the opportunity to think of really innovative ideas without those limitations. It helped us to understand what was truly possible. We were able to go back to leadership and ask for what we wanted and give them the opportunity to "counter" with what they could do. It was a practice in asking for what we wanted and negotiating for what we needed.
>
> So, give yourself the gift of thinking about your UVC without the traditional constraints.

STEP 2: REFLECTING ON YOUR CAPABILITIES

Your capabilities extend beyond skills you've been trained in. They include your natural ways of thinking, relating, and approaching challenges. In other words, the things you do well with less effort than others seem to require.

Exercise: Capability Reality Check

Grab your journal and reflect on the following capabilities:

Success Architecture: When are you at your best? Identify three professional achievements you're genuinely proud of. For each, list the specific capabilities that enabled that success. Look beyond obvious technical skills to how you approached the situation.

Your Invisible Strengths: Ask 5–7 colleagues this question: "What's the invisible strength that I bring? What do I consistently do well that others in similar roles might approach differently?" Look for patterns in their responses.

Flow Experiences: When do you lose track of time because you're absorbed in your work? These "flow states" often indicate activities that align with your natural capabilities. If nothing comes to mind immediately, that's okay! Look out for flow experiences in your daily work and make note of them.

Early Indicators: What activities came naturally to you from an early age? These long-standing patterns often reveal innate capabilities rather than just acquired skills.

After gathering this information, identify 3–5 capabilities that consistently appear in your analysis. Express these as action phrases like "synthesizing complex information," "building consensus across different perspectives," or "anticipating implementation challenges."

STEP 3: FORMULATING YOUR IMPACT STATEMENT (UVC FORMULATION)

Finally, distill your intersection analysis into a concise UVC statement that captures the essence of your unique contribution. This statement should explain how you make a difference or how you impact others. This statement should:

- Feel energizing and good in your body when you read it.
- Include both what you do and why or how you approach it.
- Connect to work that creates value for your organization.
- Be specific enough that it highlights what sets you apart from others doing similar work.

Here are examples from three different professionals:

Financial Analyst UVC: "I transform complex financial data into clear insights that empower non-financial colleagues to make confident decisions, promoting both analytical rigor and inclusive understanding."

HR Director UVC: "I design people systems that balance organizational needs with individual dignity, creating structures that simultaneously enhance performance, fairness, and human development."

Marketing Manager UVC: "I translate brand values into practical customer experiences by anticipating unstated needs and creating solutions that feel both innovative and intuitively right."

Note how each UVC statement connects values (what matters) with capabilities (what they do well) in ways that create distinctive value. In other words, these are individual signatures of their professional contributions.

>  **TRUTH BOMB**
>
> Your UVC gives you both the clarity and the flexibility to achieve balance between what you value and what you do especially well. When you understand what makes your contribution truly distinctive, you can adapt how you express it without compromising who you fundamentally are.

Once you've clearly articulated your UVC, you have a powerful tool for navigating any organizational culture without losing yourself.

Your UVC becomes:

A Decision Filter: When faced with different approaches to a task or role, choose the one that best allows you to express your UVC.

A Communication Guide: Frame your ideas and contributions in ways that highlight the distinctive value your UVC brings to situations.

A Development Focus: Rather than trying to improve in every possible area, focus your growth efforts on enhancing the capabilities central to your UVC.

A Negotiation Framework: When discussing role changes or new responsibilities, advocate for assignments that align with your UVC while addressing organizational needs.

When Marcus, the finance executive I mentioned earlier, formulated his UVC as "I bridge financial expertise and operational realities, creating mutual understanding that enables better-informed decisions," it gave him a clear framework for reshaping his role. He didn't have to choose between fitting in as a traditional financial analyst and being true to his natural strengths as a translator between departments.

Your UVC as Your North Star

Throughout your career journey, your UVC remains your authentic center, a guiding constellation that helps you navigate changing landscapes while remaining true to yourself.

By understanding, communicating, applying, and evolving your Unique Values and Capabilities, you transform the challenge of "fitting in without losing yourself" into an opportunity to make your most meaningful contribution. You discover that the question isn't whether to adapt or remain true to yourself — it's how to express your authentic self in ways that create value in each new context.

The most successful professionals are those who maintain a clear sense of their distinctive contribution while continually finding fresh, relevant ways to express it, creating value for their organizations while experiencing the deep satisfaction that comes from doing work that truly reflects who they are.

My maternal grandmother, Agatha Schroeder, was a force of nature who lived to be 106 years old. What made her truly remarkable wasn't just her longevity, though; it was her refusal to accept limitations based on age or circumstance. At 63, when most people are thinking about retirement, she earned her degree in nursing.

I'll never forget asking her, "Miss Agie, what's your secret?" Her response has stayed with me ever since: "I don't operate with an expiration date. There's no finish line for growth."

She embodied this philosophy until her final days. While others saw age as a barrier, she saw each new day as simply another chapter in her continuous journey of learning and contributing. Her example taught me that you don't have to put artificial finish lines or expiration dates on your personal development. Growth is indeed continuous... if you choose to embrace it.

Miss Agie's wisdom reminds me that excellence is about maintaining the curiosity and courage to keep evolving, regardless of where you are in life.

Remember: Your UVC will continue to grow, amplify, and elevate your personal brand and career. To make this happen, though, it's important to avoid imposing restrictions like, "by this date or year, I must be doing this…" Focus instead on how you can use your voice to communicate your value. Your voice is your most valuable asset. When you own your voice as your superpower, you don't just advance your career — you create space for others to do the same.

Your UVC is the bridge between who you are and the impact you create. By developing this bridge thoughtfully over time, you ensure that belonging never requires losing yourself, but rather finding ever more powerful ways to bring your unique contribution to every environment you enter.

Chapter 4
Unleashing Your Signature Communication Style

"Don't waste your time trying to explain yourself to people that are committed to misunderstanding you."

— Shannon L. Alder, author and therapist

When Alicia was promoted to lead a team at a major healthcare organization, she thought she had "made it." With her impressive credentials, technical knowledge, and consistent ability to meet deadlines, she assumed her career would continue its upward trajectory. But six months into her new role, her supervisor pulled her aside: "You're doing the job, but you're not standing out. I need you to be more visible, more influential."

Alicia was stunned. She had always believed that doing good work would speak for itself. This is the Competence Trap in action. Alicia's skills and competence led to her promotion, and now she was discovering that technical excellence alone wasn't enough to advance further. The truth hit her hard: what got her to this position wouldn't get her where she wanted to go next.

This scenario plays out daily across organizations of all sizes. Professionals like Alicia discover that excelling at required tasks is merely the baseline expectation. To truly advance, especially in today's AI-powered landscape, you must develop something algorithms can't replicate: a signature communication style that makes you irreplaceable.

Take a moment to think about your own workplace. You know those people—the ones who maybe weren't the strongest technical performers but somehow kept getting promoted while more skilled colleagues got overlooked. What did they have that others didn't?

They understood something crucial: they knew how to communicate their value in ways that resonated with decision makers.

THE PIE THEORY: PERFORMANCE, IMAGE, AND EXPOSURE

I first learned about the PIE Theory when I was at GE. Harvey Coleman's research[34] revealed something that shocked many high performers: your job performance accounts for only 10% of your career advancement. Let that sink in for a moment.

The other 90%? That's all about how you communicate your value.

Performance (10%): Your Entry Ticket Performance is essential — it's your baseline credibility. You have to deliver results consistently. But here's the reality check: in most organizations, everyone at your level can do the job. Performance gets you in the game, but it won't differentiate you from your peers.

Image (30%): How Others See Your Potential Your image isn't about being fake or putting on a show. It's about how consistently you demonstrate your capabilities, professionalism, and leadership potential. As Coleman puts it: "You get paid on performance, you get promoted on what other people think of your potential." This is where the way you communicate, the way you handle challenges, and the way you show up in meetings matters tremendously.

Exposure (60%): Making Your Value Visible This is the big one, and it's where most people like Alicia get stuck. You can't assume that excellent work will speak for itself. You need the right people to see you in action, understand your contributions,

---

[34] "The PIE Theory: Performance, Image, and Exposure in Career Progression," *The Networking Institute*, July 21, 2023 (https://thenetworkinginstitute.com/media/networking/the-pie-theory-performance-image-and-exposure-in-career-progression/#:~:text=Today%2C%20we'll%20explore%20the,in%20shaping%20your%20professional%20advancement).

and recognize your potential. This means strategically building relationships, volunteering for visible projects, and learning to articulate your impact in terms that resonate with decision makers.

I've watched this pattern play out countless times. The person who gets the promotion isn't always the one with the most impressive spreadsheet or the cleanest code. It's the one who can walk into a room and make their contributions feel essential. They speak the language that leadership understands. They frame their work in terms of business impact. They build relationships that extend beyond their immediate team. Most importantly, they don't wait for their work to speak for itself; they become the voice that makes their work impossible to ignore.

> **TIME OUT**
>
> Yep. I'm reading your mind again. This time, you're thinking I might be asking you to perform, and you might be wondering if all that talk about creating a culture of genuine connection was, well... all talk.
>
> Unleashing your signature communication style isn't about playing politics or being fake, though. It's about recognizing that in today's workplace, your ability to communicate your unique value is just as important as creating that value in the first place.
>
> I know this can be frustrating if you're the type who prefers to keep your head down and do the work. Believe me when I tell you, I'm not asking you to become the loudest one in the room. There are ways to strategically tout your own work without getting a full personality makeover.

Next, we'll explore how to apply your UVC in environments where you feel like an outsider, leveraging your unique perspective to create value rather than simply trying to conform or withdraw. This is where your UVC truly becomes your career superpower.

Turning "Otherness" into Opportunity: Your UVC in Challenging Environments

When you experience being "the only one in a room," these situations where you feel visibly different often create pressure to choose one of two paths: either you overcompensate or you withdraw. It's a classic fight or flight response.

I used to believe that being the loudest in the room meant that you were the most impactful. And I know I'm not alone. We are conditioned, especially as ambitious go-getters, to perceive verbal dominance as leadership. But successful leaders understand that quieter, more introverted team members aren't less engaged. They have different, but equally valuable, capabilities. These individuals are often listening deeply, analyzing thoroughly, and formulating comprehensive responses while others are busy talking over each other.

I call these people the "quiet storms," and I'll be honest — I used to see soft-spoken or quiet team members as disengaged. That was a huge mistake on my part, and it goes back to the principle that you can't expect you from others. I used to associate being a powerful leader with being loud and outspoken because that's what I saw (and I know I'm not alone in this).

Growing up as an only child in a small rural town, I believed that if you could out-talk, out-debate, and out-shine everyone else, you'd win. During those formative years, I was always "the only one" in whatever room I entered, so I felt like I had to prove myself. That's where I developed this mindset: I can out-talk, out-debate, out-shine everybody else. Anytime I entered a room where I was the only one, I'd activate that part ("Go, Go Gadget Overcompensation"). As a result of this mindset, if you were quiet, I regarded you as weak.

But as time went on, I learned that being powerful or impactful as a leader doesn't have to announce itself. It's something that should be felt, not heard. When you're in rooms full of high performers — and you know I spent years in Fortune 100 companies — everybody has something to say. Everyone's competitive, everyone's driven by ego. I always felt like I had to match that energy by out-talking and out-debating everyone else. But this strategy doesn't work as well in these environments.

Over the last five years especially, I've been quicker to listen, to observe, and to really appreciate those who do the same. Quiet people are processors. Even though they're not loud with their ideas, they usually are the ones with the most impactful ideas, since they listen more than they talk. For those who are the quiet ones in rooms, sometimes their quietness is actually a strength. The loudest voice isn't always the strongest. The strongest voice might be the one that whispers but still rattles or shifts the room.

Okay, so what do you do if you're the quiet storm? If you're an introverted professional in a predominantly extroverted environment, it's critical you level-set with colleagues, since they may not know how to read you. For example, you could say something like this: "I want to level-set with you about my communication style. Just because I don't talk all the time doesn't mean I'm not engaged. I'm a listener and a processor. If you stop seeing great work from me after these meetings, I welcome a conversation about that. Until then, embrace that I'm different but just as powerful."

Remember, perception is reality in professional settings. If you don't explain your communication style to others, they'll create their own narrative about your participation. Instead of feeling defeated, powerless, or outnumbered in these situations, use your voice as your superpower. Find a way to share in a professional, non-defensive way that you listen to learn, while others might be listening only to respond. This is an opportunity for you to steer the narrative.

Your UVC offers a path beyond either (awkwardly) mimicking the dominant style or withdrawing entirely. It provides the foundation for strategic belonging that transforms perceived "otherness" into distinctive value.

Following are some constructive ways to put your UVC to work in challenging environments:

REFRAME DIFFERENCE AS PERSPECTIVE

The first step in applying your UVC in environments where you feel like an outsider is to reframe how you think about your differences. What initially feels like being "other" can actually represent a valuable vantage point.

As we saw above, it can be as simple as telling people "I'm a listener" or "I'm a processor" when you realize you're in an alpha-dominant culture with people who assume you're not engaged. Follow James's lead, for example. James, a soft-spoken analytical thinker working in a sales organization full of gregarious personalities, initially tried to force himself into an extroverted communication style that felt exhausting and fake. Through our work together, he identified his UVC as "I create thoughtful, evidence-based solutions that balance enthusiasm with feasibility, helping turn exciting possibilities into achievable realities."

Rather than viewing his analytical approach as a limitation in a high-energy sales culture, James began positioning it as a complementary strength. In planning meetings, while his colleagues generated ambitious revenue targets, he would say: "My strength is creating the bridge between our aspirations and execution. Let me outline how we might structure this approach to maximize our chances of success."

By explicitly connecting his different perspective to value creation, James transformed how his contributions were received. His colleagues began seeking his input earlier in the planning process, and his influence grew—not despite his difference, but because of how he leveraged it.

TEACH PEOPLE HOW TO TREAT YOU

When you understand your UVC clearly, you can be more strategic about how and when to share aspects of your authentic self. Think of your job here as thoughtfully choosing which elements of your perspective to emphasize in different contexts.

Elena, a senior leader who grew up in significantly different socioeconomic circumstances than most of her executive peers, felt like an outsider in conversations peppered with references to exclusive experiences she hadn't shared. After identifying her UVC as "I create inclusive solutions by connecting diverse perspectives, ensuring we address problems from multiple angles rather than defaulting to conventional approaches," she began selectively sharing her background when it offered relevant perspective.

In a discussion about a product aimed at budget-conscious consumers, she might say: "My perspective may be useful here. Having grown up in a household where every purchase was carefully weighed, I see some assumptions in our marketing materials that might not match the reality of our target customers."

By connecting her personal experience directly to business value rather than sharing it as an isolated fact about herself, Elena helped her colleagues see her different perspective as an asset rather than something that made her "other."

PLAY TO YOUR STRENGTHS IN DIFFERENT SETTINGS

Your UVC likely encompasses multiple capabilities that you can emphasize differently depending on the environment. This flexibility allows you to remain authentic while adapting to different contexts. Did you catch that? Yep, we're talking about adaptability again. See, I told you that was a critical strength.

Again, Marcus, whose UVC centered on "bridging financial expertise and operational realities," emphasized different aspects of this contribution in different settings. With finance colleagues, he highlighted his ability to translate technical concepts for non-financial audiences, positioning himself as the team's ambassador. With operational leaders, he emphasized his financial expertise while acknowledging the practical constraints they faced, becoming their trusted advisor in navigating financial requirements.

By flexibly emphasizing different aspects of his UVC rather than trying to be someone he wasn't, Marcus maintained his authenticity while building strong relationships across the organization.

CREATE VALUE THROUGH CONTRAST

The most powerful application of your UVC in environments where you feel different is to explicitly create value through the contrast between your perspective and the dominant view.

Lin, the only professional with design experience on an engineering-heavy product team, initially felt her aesthetic considerations were dismissed as subjective or secondary. After clarifying her UVC as "I integrate human-centered design principles with technical functionality, creating solutions that people intuitively understand and enjoy using," she began to see more clearly how her difference could become an asset to the team.

Rather than presenting her design input as a counterpoint to engineering considerations, she positioned it as a complementary perspective: "While we've thoroughly addressed the technical requirements, adding this design approach will significantly enhance user adoption. My experience with similar interfaces suggests that this adjustment would reduce support calls by approximately 30%."

By explicitly connecting her different perspective to outcomes the team valued, Lin transformed potential conflict into valuable contrast. Over time, the team began proactively seeking her input earlier in the development process.

When to Speak Up for Change

Sometimes the adaptability ball doesn't *just* fall in your court. Applying your UVC in challenging environments can reveal a legitimate need for cultural evolution. Your unique perspective may help you identify dysfunctional patterns that others have normalized. It's kind of like having x-ray vision!

When you encounter systemic barriers to expressing your UVC, consider whether the issue warrants advocacy for change.

Ask yourself:

- Does this barrier impact only me, or does it likely affect others as well?
- Is the barrier inconsistent with the organization's stated values or objectives?
- Would addressing this barrier create value beyond my personal comfort?

If you determine that advocacy is appropriate, approach it through the lens of your UVC rather than personal accommodation. For example, instead of going to your supervisor and saying "I need this process changed because it doesn't work for me," you might say, "I've noticed this approach creates challenges for people with different communication styles, potentially causing us to miss valuable insights. Here's an alternative that might help us benefit from more diverse perspectives."

By framing advocacy in terms of organizational benefit rather than personal exception, you increase the likelihood of meaningful change. Plus, you increase the value of your own communication currency.

INTENTION VS. IMPACT: COMMUNICATION THAT WORKS

One of my core beliefs is that there are more good people in this world than not. In other words, most people have the best intentions at heart. In general, this means that we should assume that people are good until they show us otherwise. Specifically, when overcoming common communication barriers, we should focus on intention, rather than impact.

As someone who may have been interrupted, dismissed, or criticized, you can make the other person aware by saying: "I'm not sure what you meant when you interrupted me, but it made me feel dismissed, and I wanted to bring that to your attention because I may have misinterpreted it."

We live in a world right now where people are afraid to speak because they are worried about saying the wrong thing. What we have to get back to, as part of owning our superpower through communication, is teaching people how to treat us.

This approach means shining a light on what you observe with the purpose of increasing clarity. When you help others understand that despite their good intentions, their impact wasn't what they intended, you build the foundation for genuine connection and mutual respect.

In the next section, we'll explore how to communicate your UVC effectively to others, ensuring that your unique contributions are recognized and valued even in environments where you initially feel like an outsider.

Making Your Value Known: Ensuring Your UVC Gets Recognized

Understanding your Unique Values and Capabilities (UVC) is half the equation. For your UVC to create impact, others must recognize and value your distinctive contribution. You own this. Owning your UVC becomes especially critical in environments where you already feel like an outsider, where your perspective might be overlooked or misinterpreted.

I recall one time when I joined a team of leadership facilitators. I was new to the team and invited to coach a group of business leaders — senior managers and C-suite. One of the other facilitators, who had been on the team for years, stood up and introduced me. When he did, he laid out my credentials well and did a generally fabulous job, except for one thing: he called me an "emerging leader." As soon as the words came out of his mouth, I said, "Let me stop you there." I looked each of the senior leaders sitting across the table in the eye and I said, "I'm an established leader ready to help each of you."

This is what effective self-advocacy looks like in action. Too often, we let others define our narrative, especially when we're new to a team or organization. Colleagues might say things like "you've only been in your role for a year" or label you as "emerging" when you bring decades of relevant experience. I used to get that every time I started in a new position. The key is to immediately remind people of your previous experience and how it directly applies to the current situation. In this moment, I was positioning myself to bring different perspectives and insights that would help us exceed desired outcomes and expectations (not simply correcting an inaccurate label).

At the end of the session, there was a poll to see which leaders wanted to work with which coach and most leaders chose me. Do you know why this happened? It happened because I showed those leaders that my voice is valuable. By advocating for myself in that moment, I connected the dots between my experience and their needs.

After the session, I also pulled the facilitator aside, without being defensive (I assume the best intentions from everyone, remember?) and graciously said, "In the future, let's align on how we introduce one another." I didn't use a negative or scolding tone. I didn't raise hell or come across as a stereotypical angry Black woman. I simply made it clear that we should be in control of our narratives. This is the reason self-advocacy is so important versus waiting on someone else to recognize our value.

The challenge lies in communicating your UVC without appearing either arrogant or apologetic. Next, let's explore practical strategies to help others see and appreciate your unique value.

THE FRAME-DEMONSTRATE-REINFORCE CYCLE

Effective UVC communication follows a three-part cycle that builds recognition over time:

1. **Frame** your contribution before delivering it, helping others understand how to interpret what you'll offer.
2. **Demonstrate** your UVC through consistent action that creates visible value.
3. **Reinforce** connections between your contributions and positive outcomes, helping others recognize patterns in your impact.

Let's examine each component in detail.

1. Strategic Framing

Framing prepares others to receive your contribution by establishing context and expectations. Think simple here. Often a single sentence can effectively position your perspective better than a more elaborate explanation.

Maria, a product manager with a UVC centered on "integrating diverse user perspectives to create inclusive solutions," used framing effectively when joining discussions dominated by technical considerations:

"Before we finalize this feature set, I'd like to share insights from our accessibility research that might influence our priorities."

This simple framing accomplished several important goals:

- It signaled her unique perspective before sharing it.
- It connected her contribution to the team's objectives.
- It established why others should value her different viewpoint.

Contrast this with diving directly into accessibility concerns without context, which might have been perceived as derailing the technical discussion rather than enhancing it.

EFFECTIVE FRAMING STRUCTURES

Effective framing statements often follow this structure:

1. Acknowledge the current focus
2. Signal your distinctive perspective
3. Connect it to shared objectives

For example:

- "Building on our revenue analysis, I'd like to examine how these numbers translate to operational realities, which might affect our implementation timeline."
- "As we consider technical solutions, I can offer perspective on how similar approaches have affected team collaboration in my previous experience."

> - "Now that we've established our target metrics, I'd like to explore how we might communicate them in ways that resonate with different learning styles across our teams."

2. Consistent Demonstration

While framing sets expectations, demonstration delivers on them through consistent action that creates recognizable value. This is where your UVC moves from concept to impact.

Michael, whose UVC centered on "translating strategic objectives into practical implementation steps," demonstrated this capability consistently in cross-functional meetings by:

- Creating simple visual roadmaps that clarified complex initiatives;
- Identifying potential execution barriers others hadn't considered; and
- Suggesting concrete first steps when discussions became too abstract.

He didn't need to verbally claim this as his strength; his consistent contributions made the pattern clear to others.

> **EFFECTIVE DEMONSTRATION STRUCTURES**
>
> Effective demonstration requires:
>
> **Consistency:** Apply your UVC regularly, not just in high-visibility moments.
>
> **Relevance:** Ensure your contributions address current priorities rather than showcasing your strengths regardless of context.
>
> **Adaptability:** Adjust how you express your UVC based on the situation while maintaining its core essence.
>
> **Quality over quantity:** Deliver high-value contributions aligned with your UVC rather than attempting to contribute in every possible way.

3. Tactical Reinforcement

Reinforcement helps others connect your contributions to positive outcomes, strengthening recognition of your UVC over time. This means helping others see patterns in how your distinctive approach creates value.

Alisha, whose UVC involved "identifying unspoken concerns that might derail consensus," used reinforcement effectively after a successful product launch:

"I'm glad the team took time to address the distribution team's concerns before finalizing the packaging design. That extra week of discussion prevented what could have been costly rework later."

This subtle reinforcement reminded others of her contribution without claiming individual credit for the outcome.

EFFECTIVE REINFORCEMENT STRUCTURES

Effective reinforcement approaches include:

Outcome connections: "Our approach of involving customer service early in the design process seems to have paid off in the reduced support calls we're seeing."

Process reflections: "Taking the extra time for inclusive brainstorming gave us perspectives we might have missed with our usual approach."

Future applications: "Given how well the cross-functional review worked for this project, we might want to build that into our standard process."

Recognition redirection: When praised individually, acknowledge others while subtly reinforcing the value of your distinctive approach: "Thanks! I think what made the difference was ensuring we had representation from all user groups in our testing phase."

ADAPTING YOUR COMMUNICATION STYLE WITHOUT LOSING YOUR SOUL

Communicating your UVC effectively sometimes requires adjusting your natural communication style to ensure your message resonates. Adaptation is about ensuring your distinctive value isn't lost in translation.

Consider these adjustments for different environments:

In analytical cultures: Support your unique perspective with data and concrete examples. Connect your insights to measurable outcomes whenever possible.

In relationship-focused cultures: Build personal connections before emphasizing your distinctive contributions. Frame your UVC in terms of how it helps others or strengthens the team.

In fast-paced environments: Lead with your conclusion or recommendation, then provide supporting context only if needed. Keep reinforcement brief and results-focused.

In consensus-driven cultures: Present your unique perspective as an addition to existing views rather than a correction. Use inclusive language that builds on others' contributions.

When Kim, an operations specialist whose UVC centered on "creating systematic approaches that balance efficiency with employee well-being," joined a sales-driven organization that valued quick results over process, she adjusted her communication without abandoning her core contribution.

Instead of detailed process explanations, she began presenting "3-point implementation plans" that highlighted outcomes first, followed by streamlined steps. She still delivered her systematic approach but packaged it in a format that resonated within a results-oriented culture.

Handling Communication Roadblocks

Even with effective framing, demonstration, and reinforcement, you may encounter barriers to having your UVC recognized.

Above all, I want you to adopt this mantra: *Enter with confidence. Assume good intentions.*

When you approach people with the mindset that they have the best intentions, it sets you up to have the greatest impact. Too often, we're afraid to speak up when we feel dismissed or slighted, but if we give grace in those moments, we can teach others how to treat us.

I was at one of the world's largest airports when I noticed an elderly white woman, who appeared to be in her late eighties or early nineties, clearly struggling. She had a gift shop bag, luggage, and was on the phone telling whoever was on the other end, "I don't know if I can carry all of this."

I approached her and offered to help. While still on her call, she said to the person, "This nice colored girl offered to help me." A few other people nearby overheard and shot me looks — the kind that said they were offended on my behalf.

But I wasn't offended. This moment reminded me of my own Black grandmother calling me in high school to complain about "these colored boys leaving garbage in my yard." When you know the person or understand where they're coming from, their conditioning and the era they were socialized in, you can see past the language to the intention.

This woman wasn't trying to demean me. She was grateful and speaking in the language of her generation. Yet I watched other people looking for reasons to be outraged instead of recognizing a coachable moment.

 **TRUTH BOMB**

Sometimes the most powerful response isn't cancellation; it's understanding where people are coming from and meeting them there.

Scripts: Common Communication Roadblocks

Communication Roadblock	Recommended Response
When you're interrupted or spoken over	Instead of withdrawing or becoming confrontational, try reconnection statements: "I'd like to finish my thought about the implementation timeline, which addresses the concern Jason just raised."
When your contribution is attributed to others	Address it constructively in the moment: "Thanks for highlighting that point about user accessibility. I'm glad you found the research I shared last week valuable. I'd like to build on that by suggesting…"
When your perspective is dismissed	Seek to understand the resistance before pushing harder: "I notice there's hesitation about prioritizing user experience testing. Can you help me understand your concerns so I can better address them?" You can also be more direct by saying, "I'm not sure what you meant, but it made me feel dismissed. I wanted to make you aware that…"
When your style is criticized	Separate style criticism from the value of your contribution: "I understand my communication style might be more detailed than what you're used to. I'm working on adapting while ensuring we don't miss critical implementation factors."

BUILDING YOUR VILLAGE

You've probably heard the proverb that many argue has its roots in African culture saying, "it takes a village." I want you to keep this in mind as you learn to voice your UVC. Creating broader recognition for your UVC often requires support beyond your immediate team. Consider developing a network of allies who understand and can amplify your unique contribution:

Peer advocates who can reference your contributions in your absence: "This reminds me of what Sara was saying about considering cross-departmental impacts."

Leadership sponsors who can create opportunities for your UVC to shine: "Brian's perspective would be valuable for this initiative given his experience bridging technical and customer considerations."

Cross-functional partners who benefit directly from your unique approach and can provide testimonials to its value.

Kevin, a legal counsel with a UVC focused on "translating regulatory requirements into business-enabling frameworks," strategically built relationships with product developers who came to value his approach of finding compliant paths forward rather than simply identifying risks. These partners became his strongest advocates, often telling others, "Get Kevin involved early. He'll help you find a way to achieve your goals while managing our legal exposure."

MAKING YOUR UVC VISIBLE IN VIRTUAL ENVIRONMENTS

As remote and hybrid work becomes increasingly common, communicating your UVC effectively in virtual environments requires additional intentionality:

Make your thinking visible by sharing brief thought processes, not just conclusions: "I approached this challenge by first examining customer review patterns, then considering implementation constraints, which led me to recommend…" It's just like math class when you were a kid. You have to show your work.

Use visual reinforcement by sharing models, frameworks, or simple diagrams that represent your unique approach, making your contribution more memorable.

Create artifacts that embody your UVC — summaries, templates, or tools that others can use even when you're not present.

Leverage chat and collaborative documents to contribute your perspective in multiple formats, accommodating different communication preferences.

MEASURING YOUR IMPACT

How do you know if others truly recognize and value your UVC? Look for these indicators:

Proactive inclusion: You're invited into discussions specifically for your unique perspective.

Language adoption: Others begin using terms or frameworks you've introduced.

Referrals: You receive requests to contribute to initiatives based on others' recommendations.

Recognition alignment: Performance reviews specifically mention the unique value you articulated in your UVC.

When these indicators appear, you'll know that your UVC is becoming a recognized and valued part of your professional identity.

In our final section, we'll explore how to evolve your UVC over time as you grow professionally and as organizational needs change, ensuring that your unique contribution remains both personally authentic and externally valuable.

Evolving Your UVC: Growing Without Losing Your Core

Your Unique Values and Capabilities mature and evolve throughout your career. The most successful professionals understand how to grow their UVC organically while maintaining its authentic core. This evolution isn't about reinventing yourself with each new role or trend, but rather developing your distinctive contribution to remain relevant and impactful as both you and your organization change.

THE NATURAL EVOLUTION OF YOUR UVC

Consider how your UVC naturally evolves across career stages. In my e-learning courses, we talk about Unique Values and Capabilities at each stage (for more information, check out https://realcommcoach.com/map-my-effective-communication-journey).

Early Career (Nexus): Your UVC often emerges in its raw form. You notice certain types of opportunities to contribute come naturally and generate positive recognition. At this stage, your unique approach may be more intuitive than intentional.

Mid-Career (Trailblazer): As you gain experience, your UVC becomes more refined and deliberate. You develop systematic approaches to applying your unique strengths and become more selective about where and how you contribute.

Senior Career (Paramount): Your fully mature UVC often expands to include developing these capabilities in others. Your impact multiplies as you help teams and organizations benefit from approaches similar to your own.

Claire's UVC centered around "translating complex technical requirements into clear implementation paths that diverse team members can follow." As she progressed from technical specialist to project manager to divisional director, this core didn't change, but how she expressed it evolved significantly:

- As a specialist, she created exceptional documentation and explanations.
- As a project manager, she built processes that improved cross-functional understanding.
- As a director, she developed communication frameworks that entire departments adopted and she mentored other leaders in bridging technical and operational divides.

Throughout this progression, Claire remained authentic to her core values and capabilities while expanding their application and impact.

INTENTIONAL UVC DEVELOPMENT

While your UVC will evolve naturally over time, you can also intentionally develop it through the following methods:

Depth Expansion: Becoming even more skilled in your core capabilities. If your UVC involves "synthesizing diverse perspectives into cohesive strategies," you might deepen this by studying formal synthesis methodologies or developing more sophisticated frameworks for integration.

Scope Extension: Applying your UVC to new contexts or challenges. If you've successfully applied your UVC in marketing contexts, you might extend it to product development or organizational design.

Impact Elevation: Increasing the level at which your UVC creates value, from individual to team to organizational to industry.

Complementary Skill Building: Adding capabilities that enhance your core UVC without diluting it. If your UVC centers on innovative problem-solving, adding project management skills might help you implement those innovations more effectively.

The key is developing in ways that strengthen rather than dilute your distinctive contribution. Instead of trying to eliminate weaknesses or become well-rounded, focus on becoming exceptional in the areas central to your UVC while building just enough competence in other areas to enable your success.

ADAPTING TO ORGANIZATIONAL CHANGE

Organizations constantly evolve — priorities shift, cultures transform, and new challenges emerge. These changes can either threaten your UVC's relevance or create opportunities to apply it in valuable new ways.

When facing organizational change, ask yourself:

1. How might my UVC address emerging challenges or priorities?
2. What aspects of my UVC become more valuable in this new context?
3. How can I frame my distinctive contribution to connect with evolving needs?

Cathy, whose UVC involved "creating systems that balance procedural consistency with human needs," initially felt threatened when her organization announced a major digital transformation initiative focused on automation. Instead of resisting the change, she reframed her contribution: "As we automate processes, my focus will be ensuring our systems complement rather than constrain human work, maximizing both efficiency and employee experience."

By connecting her enduring UVC to the organization's new direction, Cathy positioned herself as a valuable contributor to change rather than an obstacle to it.

Cathy shows how important verbal communication can be when you're in the midst of organizational change. When I worked at Stonehaven , they went through a big transition, which you'll hear more about in Chapter 7 (but please don't skip ahead because the rest of this chapter and the next three are super important!). In that role, especially with what the organization went through, my UVC positioned me well to be an asset to the leadership team. I know how to bring together the right people to make critical decisions, and in the midst of change, decision-making is job number one.

If you find yourself in a similar position, meet with your leader to make them aware of your UVC and how you can be an asset to help them navigate the change. You'll be strengthening a relationship while developing yourself — a win-win!

WHEN TO EVOLVE VS. WHEN TO MOVE ON

As important as it is to be adaptive, sometimes organizational changes create environments where your UVC simply cannot thrive. Before concluding you need to leave, consider these adaptation strategies:

Role Crafting: Negotiate to reshape aspects of your current role to better align with your UVC while still meeting organizational needs.

Internal Mobility: Look for roles or projects within your organization where your UVC would create more obvious value.

Contribution Reframing: Identify new ways your existing UVC addresses emerging priorities or challenges.

If these approaches don't create sufficient alignment, it may be time to seek environments where your UVC can create greater impact. Remember: leaving isn't failing. It's recognizing that both you and the organization will benefit from better alignment between your distinctive contribution and organizational needs.

Passing On Your UVC: Teaching Others Your Superpower

As your career advances, one of the most powerful ways to extend your impact is by helping others develop capabilities similar to yours. This means sharing approaches and perspectives that others can integrate into their own authentic contributions (not creating clones).

Effective UVC teaching includes:

Explicit Process Sharing: Articulating your approaches rather than just demonstrating them. For example, when I'm coaching a client through a difficult conversation, I first help them identify their emotional triggers, then we clarify their core message, and finally we practice delivery techniques that align with their authentic communication style.

Mentoring: Providing ongoing guidance to help others develop similar capabilities while finding their own authentic expression.

Creating Frameworks: Developing tools, templates, or methodologies that allow others to apply aspects of your approach independently.

Celebrating Diverse Expressions: Recognizing that others will incorporate your teachings into their own UVC in unique ways rather than replicating yours exactly.

By teaching elements of your UVC, you multiply your impact while often discovering new dimensions of your own contribution through the teaching process itself.

YOUR LEGACY BEYOND YOU

As you approach career maturity, consider how your UVC might create lasting impact beyond your direct involvement:

Institutional Practices: How might approaches flowing from your UVC become standard practices within your organization?

Knowledge Transfer: What aspects of your unique approach should be documented or formalized for others to reference?

Culture Shaping: How has your consistent demonstration of your UVC influenced the values and practices of teams you've led?

Succession Development: Who demonstrates potential to carry forward aspects of your distinctive contribution after you move on?

Building this legacy happens through consistent application of your UVC over time, deliberate knowledge sharing, and intentional development of others.

Your Brand: Beyond Corporate Identity

"But I work for a large company — I don't need a personal brand."

I hear this (or some version of this) misconception frequently from clients. Let me be clear: *you are a brand*. From the moment you wake up and engage to the time you go to bed to wind down, everyone experiences your brand. Your organization has a brand, your department has a culture, and you need a distinct identity within that ecosystem.

Your personal brand is the unique value you bring to every conversation, meeting, and interaction. It's how people experience you when you communicate. It's the impression you leave behind, the way colleagues describe you to others, and ultimately, what makes you memorable in a sea of qualified professionals.

In today's corporate environment, anonymity is a career liability.

THE POWER OF STANDING OUT

Consider this scenario I witnessed at a Fortune 100 company: Two equally qualified managers were up for the same director position. Both had impressive resumes, met their targets consistently, and had similar experience levels. The difference? One had cultivated a reputation as a clear, confident communicator who could translate complex topics into actionable insights. She was known for asking insightful questions and connecting ideas across departments.

The other manager was competent but forgettable in meetings, speaking only when necessary and blending into the corporate background. Guess who received the promotion?

Your ability to articulate your unique perspective and vision — yes, even if you haven't stepped into leadership just yet — is now a non-negotiable professional asset. This isn't about being the loudest voice or most extroverted presence. It's about being intentional with how you communicate your value.

What Got You Here Won't Get You There

Earlier, I mentioned that many professionals fall into what I call the "competence trap." They've reached their current position through technical skills, education, and consistently meeting expectations. Then they hit a ceiling, confused about why their career momentum has stalled.

> 💣 **TRUTH BOMB**
>
> The skills that propel you through early- and mid-career stages — primarily technical expertise and task completion — become less distinctive as you advance.

At higher levels, everyone has technical competence. You may find yourself in a position similar to an elite athlete who just joined a professional team. As a diehard NFL fan, I've seen the impact of personal branding watching the televised NFL draft every year. Every athlete who enters the draft has talent — the ability to perform at the highest level on the field — or else they wouldn't be there. But what differentiates the players who get drafted early from those who slip to later rounds (or don't get drafted at all) often has everything to do with how people experience them off the field. How do they engage with the media? How do they communicate during interviews? Do they demonstrate leadership qualities? Can they articulate their vision for contributing to a team?

The same principle applies in corporate environments. While you were once used to standing out for your extraordinary technical skills (e.g., maybe you were the Excel wizard in your department or the go-to problem solver on your team), now that you're running with the big dogs, everyone around you has similar capabilities. You have to find new ways to stand out from the pack. You have to become a leader instead of simply a manager.

What separates leaders from managers is their ability to:

- Articulate a compelling vision.
- Connect with diverse audiences authentically.
- Translate complex ideas into clear direction.
- Inspire action through their communication.

Just like those NFL prospects, your technical skills got you to this level, but your ability to communicate your value, build relationships, and influence others will determine how much further you can go.

I coached a brilliant engineer who couldn't understand why he kept getting passed over for leadership roles. His technical skills were unmatched, but in presentations, he overwhelmed his audience with details and failed to convey the strategic importance of his work. We worked together to develop a communication style that honored his analytical strengths while making his insights accessible to non-technical stakeholders.

Within six months of developing this signature style, he was promoted to a position that had eluded him for years. His knowledge base hadn't changed; how he communicated it had transformed.

AI-Proof Your Career

We cannot discuss communication without acknowledging how artificial intelligence is transforming the workplace quickly and in ways that aren't entirely clear to us yet. AI can generate reports, analyze data, create presentations, and even draft emails. What it cannot do is bring your unique human perspective, energy, and connection to your work.

The question becomes: How do you position yourself as irreplaceable in a world where AI can handle increasingly complex communication tasks?

MOVING BEYOND THE ALGORITHM

During a recent workshop with a team needing to adjust to how automation might change their workplace, I asked participants to list their daily tasks and essential activities. Then I had them separate the tasks into two categories: "AI-Replaceable" and "Uniquely Human." The exercise was eye-opening. Many realized that 60–70% of their routine work could potentially be automated.

However, the "Uniquely Human" column contained their most valuable contributions:

- Building trust with skeptical stakeholders
- Reading the emotional undercurrents in a tense negotiation
- Adapting communication style to different personalities
- Bringing creative solutions to unprecedented challenges
- Creating genuine connection through shared experiences

These capabilities cannot be replicated by even the most sophisticated algorithms because they require emotional intelligence, cultural awareness, and human connection.

This is a great exercise for you to do too. Start by listing your daily tasks and essential activities or track what you do each day for a week. This will give you a good starting point. Now separate the items on your list into "AI-Replaceable" and "Uniquely Human." Consider how you can drive conversation about your work toward the "Uniquely Human" column.

The AI-Human Skills Inventory: Your Career Survival Guide

Let's get real about something that keeps even the most confident professionals up at night: in a world where AI is snatching jobs faster than free donuts disappear from the breakroom (and you know I love donuts!), what makes YOU irreplaceable? This is your career survival strategy. Let's dive in.

PART 1: UNCOVER YOUR REALITY CHECK

Step 1: Track Where Your Time Actually Goes

For one week, become a detective of your own professional life. Document everything you do and how long it takes. And I mean everything — from the strategic planning session to the 20 minutes you spent formatting that PowerPoint no one will remember. This isn't about judgment; it's about seeing the unfiltered truth of your contribution.

Step 2: Sort Your Professional DNA

Now for the moment of truth. Split your list into two brutally honest columns:

"AI could do this tomorrow"	"Only a human (YOU) could do this"
Crunching those quarterly numbers	Building trust with that client who's been burned before
Generating the weekly status report	Reading the room when half the team is disengaged but won't say why
Managing your calendar chaos	Creating genuine connection through sharing an embarrassing story

"AI could do this tomorrow"	"Only a human (YOU) could do this"
Finding that email from six months ago	Adapting your communication when talking to engineers versus when talking to executives
Writing the first draft of literally anything	Coming up with solutions to problems no one's seen before

Step 3: Face the Numbers

Calculate what percentage of your time goes to each column. Brace yourself—most people discover they're spending 60–70% of their day on tasks that AI could handle while you grab coffee. Let that marinate.

PART 2: REPOSITION OR BECOME OBSOLETE

Step 4: Double Down on Your Human Superpowers

For each item in your "Only Human" column:

- Articulate how this skill makes your organization actual money or saves actual time.
- Document recent wins where this uniquely human skill made the difference.
- Identify how you could dial this up to 11 in your current role.

Step 5: Transform Your Robot-Ready Tasks

For everything in the "AI Could Do This" column:

- What technology could take this off your plate yesterday?
- How could you add a distinctly human element that transforms the value?

- If you reclaimed this time, what high-impact work would you do instead?

Step 6: Make Your Human Value Impossible to Miss

Develop your visibility strategy:

- In your next team meeting, highlight the insight you gained by noticing someone's body language shift.
- In your performance review, quantify the impact of your relationship-building skills (not just your spreadsheet skills).
- When discussing project outcomes, emphasize how your human judgment enhanced what the technology provided.

PART 3: COMMUNICATE YOUR IRREPLACEABLE VALUE

Step 7: Craft Your "Only You" Value Statement

This is the most important step. However, before you craft your "only you" value statement, you need to have the mindset that YOU are valuable. Without this mindset, the statement will sound like a script rather than a genuine approach. Who utilizes scripts? Actors. And you don't want to sound like you're acting in this case.

Write a statement that articulates what makes you irreplaceably human:

"I transform technical gobbledygook into solutions regular humans actually want by bridging the gap between our engineers' brilliant minds and our customers' unspoken frustrations. I'm the translator who ensures we build products that don't just check boxes but address what keeps people up at night."

Step 8: Arm Yourself with Stories, Not Just Stats

Develop specific examples that showcase your uniquely human superpowers in action. When someone asks what you do, skip the job title and role description. Instead, share how you resolved that impossible situation by reading subtle cues no algorithm could detect.

Step 9: Your 90-Day Human Advantage Plan

Create a concrete timeline to shift how you talk about your work, spend your time, and position your value — progressively emphasizing what makes you distinctly, irreplaceably human.

THE QUESTIONS THAT CHANGE EVERYTHING:

Which of your human superpowers brings you that "I was born for this" feeling when you use it?

1. What uniquely human contribution do others see in you that you've been undervaluing?

2. If technology handled half of your routine tasks by next quarter, how would you invest that reclaimed time to create 10 times more value?

3. What human skill do you need to level up, and who could mentor you in developing it?

4. How would leading with your human advantages (not just your technical skills) change how you introduce yourself at your next industry event?

Remember: The goal isn't to fight the AI tide — that's a losing battle. The winning strategy is to surf it by leveraging tools that handle the routine while you double down on the capabilities that make you beautifully, irreplaceably human. Your unique blend of emotional intelligence, cultural awareness, creative thinking, and relationship magic can't be replicated by algorithms — that's your competitive advantage in a world increasingly dominated by code.

BECOME UN-IGNORABLE

Your voice, both literal and figurative, is the primary vehicle for your personal brand. How you express ideas, the questions you ask, the insights you share, and the energy you bring to interactions all communicate who you are professionally.

To make yourself irreplaceable:

1. Uncover Your Communication Superpowers

What aspects of communication come naturally to you? Are you particularly skilled at:

- Explaining complex concepts simply?
- Building rapport quickly?
- Asking insightful questions?
- Mediating conflicts?
- Energizing a room?
- Active listening?

Your communication strengths form the foundation of your signature style.

2. Make Your Values Unmistakable

Effective communication flows from your core values. When you speak from your values, your communication gains conviction and consistency that cannot be replicated.

I worked with a marketing executive who struggled with public speaking until we connected his presentations to his deep value of empowering consumers. Once his communication aligned with this core value, his presentations transformed from stilted to compelling because he was speaking from conviction.

3. Develop Your Signature Perspective

What unique lens do you bring to your work? Perhaps it's cross-industry experience, diverse cultural understanding, or specialized knowledge. Whatever your distinctive perspective, it should inform how you communicate.

A client with experience in both healthcare and technology brought unique insights when she consciously incorporated both perspectives in her communications. Her ability to translate between these worlds made her an invaluable bridge in her organization — a role no AI could fulfill.

4. Create Communication Patterns That Stick

Consistency creates recognition. Whether it's your presentation structure, the metaphors you use, or your meeting facilitation style, developing recognizable patterns helps cement your personal brand.

One executive I coached became known for beginning every strategic discussion with the question, "How will this improve the customer experience?" This simple but consistent approach established her brand as customer-obsessed and became her signature conversation starter.

5. Embrace the Mess

At Kent State University's 2017 commencement, Oscar-winning actress Octavia Spencer delivered a powerful address urging graduates to embrace change and the inevitable messiness that comes with it. Reflecting on her own unpredictable path, she reminded students that growth often comes from the unexpected: "You're going to continue to evolve in unforeseen ways. You are full of complexities and wonders that haven't even begun to surface."[35]

Rather than fearing failure, Spencer framed it as a necessary teacher, one that reveals new strengths and shapes who you are. Too often, we think we must present a flawless version of ourselves to succeed, but the people who leave the greatest impact are those who can transform their setbacks into wisdom. As Yoda says, "The greatest teacher, failure is."

---

35 https://www.youtube.com/watch?v=0KW_dH_919w

>  **TRUTH BOMB**
>
> Your challenges are the stories that set you apart.

This means strategically sharing the struggles that shaped your perspective and the lessons that now guide your decisions, not oversharing or burdening others with your challenges. When you're discussing risk management, reference the project that taught you to build better contingency plans. When you're coaching a team member through a setback, draw on your own experience of bouncing back from disappointment. People don't connect with perfection; they connect with authenticity. When you embrace the mess and share how it shaped your strength, you become irreplaceable.

Put It Into Practice: Making Your Communication Unmistakably Yours

Developing your signature communication style is about amplifying your natural strengths while addressing areas for growth.

Here's a three-step process to help you begin:

Step 1: Hold Up a Mirror to Your Communication

Ask trusted colleagues or mentors:

- What communication situations do I handle most effectively?
- When have you seen me at my communicative best?
- What unique perspective do I bring to discussions?
- How would you describe my communication style in three words?

Their answers may surprise you and will provide valuable external perspective on your current brand.

Step 2: Find Your Verbal Fingerprint

Based on the audit and your self-reflection, identify 2–3 aspects of communication that could become your signature strengths. Focus on elements that:

- Feel good to you.
- Align with your values and natural style.
- Fulfill a need in your organization.
- Cannot be easily replicated by others or technology.

Step 3: Maximize Your Communication Impact

Look for opportunities to showcase your signature style in high-visibility situations. Start small by practicing during team meetings and other places that feel relatively safe. Then, once this feels like clockwork, you can consider expanding your comfort zone. If your strength is making complex ideas accessible, volunteer for cross-functional presentations. If you excel at building consensus, offer to facilitate challenging discussions.

The goal isn't to use your signature style in every interaction, but to deploy it strategically where it creates maximum value and visibility.

The Human Edge in an AI World

As we navigate an increasingly AI-enabled workplace, remember this fundamental truth: technology may replicate tasks, but it cannot replace authentic human connection. Your unique combination of experiences, perspectives, and communication approach represents your greatest professional asset.

>  **TRUTH BOMB**
>
> By developing and consistently demonstrating your signature communication style, you position yourself not merely as someone who completes tasks, but as an irreplaceable voice bringing distinctive value to your organization.

In my decades of coaching professionals across industries, I've witnessed this transformation repeatedly. When you stop trying to blend in and instead amplify what makes your communication distinctive, you find greater fulfillment in your work.

Your voice—human, values-driven, and uniquely yours—is the ultimate career insurance in a changing world. It's time to use it.

PART 3
MAKING EVERYONE MATTER

We've made some powerful progress already. Take a moment to give yourself a big high five. In Parts 1 and 2, we explored how you can leverage communication to transform your individual performance and build your leadership capacity. We dug into developing your signature communication style, owning your unique values and capabilities (UVC), and positioning yourself as irreplaceable in an AI-driven world. All of that is great, but here's the truth: Personal mastery alone won't create the transformation most organizations desperately need.

Part 3 takes us from "me" to "we" — addressing the million-dollar question: How do we create workplaces where everyone can bring their full selves to the table and do their best work?

Chapter 5, "Start Where You Are," gives you a no-BS assessment of today's workplace challenges. We'll examine that frustrating "top-down disconnect" where executives create fancy strategies that have nothing to do with ground-level realities. We'll tackle the post-pandemic social withdrawal that even the most extroverted leaders are experiencing. You'll learn how to spot cultural dysfunction before it tanks your results and evaluate your own leadership approach with the same brutal honesty you bring to organizational assessment.

Rather than offering some cookie-cutter solution that sounds good on paper but falls apart in practice, this chapter helps you begin exactly where you are, with practical approaches to modern challenges like motivating high performance without coming across as a dictator, and navigating those evolving workplace boundaries that have everyone walking on eggshells.

In Chapter 6, "Moving in the Right Direction," we explore how to transform workplace cultures through the three pillars that actually work: transparency, vulnerability, and humanity. You'll discover how transparency builds the trust essential for any meaningful change, how strategic vulnerability (not emotional dumping) accelerates connection, and how seeing the whole human in every team member creates engagement that lasts beyond your next quarterly town hall.

Beyond just changing your own behavior as a leader, you'll learn to create communication systems that ensure every voice contributes, even the quiet storms who aren't fighting to talk over everyone else in meetings. I'll give you practical approaches to breaking down those generational walls and building psychological safety through communication that doesn't change with the wind.

These chapters connect real-world practice with just enough theory to make it stick. By focusing on genuine belonging rather than check-the-box inclusion, you'll build cultures that leverage unique voices as superpowers rather than problems to solve. This foundation of belonging sets the stage for the organizational transformation we'll explore in Part 4, in which I'll show you how to drive breakthrough change through strategic relationship building and measuring what actually matters.

Whether you're leading five people or 5,000, these chapters provide your roadmap for creating cultures where communication drives actual excellence — where people don't just show up, they show up fully.

Chapter 5
Start Where You Are

> "When it comes to looking honestly at your own 'culture'—it can be like trying to see your backside in a mirror. You might ask: Do these jeans make my butt look big?"
>
> —Cynthia Forstmann, Co-founder, CultureTalk

Revisiting the themes from Chapters 1 and 2, let's dig a bit deeper into how to assess your starting point. Earlier I said that company culture is the invisible force that shapes everything your organization does. As I've navigated leadership positions over the years, I've witnessed firsthand how culture determines whether strategies succeed or fail, whether talent stays or leaves, and whether teams innovate or stagnate.

Let me share something I learned early in my career: you can have the most brilliant strategic plan in the world, but if your culture isn't aligned to support it, that plan is just expensive paperwork. This is the real-world implication of the "culture eats strategy for breakfast" quip we discussed in Chapter 1.

Assessing Your Culture

THE TOP-DOWN DISCONNECT

One of the most common challenges I encounter when working with senior leadership teams is what I call the "top-down disconnect." It happens when executives craft strategies in boardrooms that don't reflect the reality on the ground.

Recently, I worked with a multinational company that couldn't understand why their new digital transformation initiative wasn't gaining traction. Their strategic plan was sound. Their technology investments were substantial, and they were working with experts at the top of their class. Their timeline was reasonable. But when I spoke with middle managers and frontline employees, the problem became clear.

"We get a new strategic initiative every 18 months," one manager told me. "None of them stick because leadership doesn't understand what we actually need to serve our customers."

This disconnect manifests in several telltale ways:

- Decisions made at the top with minimal input from those who implement them.
- Decisions made at the top with minimal input from those who will be impacted.
- Leaders who rarely interact with employees beyond their direct reports.
- Communication that flows predominantly downward, not upward.
- Employees who perform tasks without understanding their purpose.
- Metrics that measure activity rather than meaningful outcomes.

Is your organization experiencing a similar disconnect?

If you're a leader, ask yourself: When was the last time you walked the floor, sat with your customer service team, or solicited honest assessment from employees without your title or position influencing their responses?

SIGNS OF CULTURAL DYSFUNCTION

Culture reveals itself in how people behave when no one is watching and in the small, everyday interactions that rarely make it into strategic plans.

Here are the warning signs of cultural dysfunction consistently observe:

High turnover in specific departments: When certain teams consistently lose good people while others retain them, it's often about leadership and culture, not compensation or the work itself.

Silence in meetings: When only senior voices speak while others remain quiet, you're missing perspectives and likely fostering resentment under the surface.

Decision paralysis: When teams need multiple approvals for minor decisions, it signals a lack of trust and empowerment. It also slows progress.

Information hoarding: When knowledge becomes currency (communication is currency!) and people protect rather than share it, collaboration suffers.

Celebration of heroics: When you regularly need "heroes" to save projects or serve customers, your processes aren't working. One of the key components of exceptional leadership is to create heroes, not be the hero.

Communication shutdown: When people avoid giving honest input because "nothing changes anyway," disengagement follows.

Note: You may have noticed that I don't use the word "feedback." I see it as a curse word. Why? I'm saving that for the next book.

Earlier I mentioned that I worked with the Wisconsin LGBTQ+ Chamber of Commerce, which experienced rapid turnover after implementing gender-inclusive restrooms and pronoun usage policies. On paper, these changes should have improved inclusion. In practice, they revealed deeper cultural challenges. Some long-term employees felt the changes were "forced" without adequate discussion, while newer employees perceived the resistance as revealing an unwelcoming environment.

However, the problem wasn't the policies. It was the implementation approach that failed to bring everyone along through effective communication. This was definitely a red flag.

Assessing Your Leadership

Culture starts with leadership. Before taking out your magnifying glass and looking closely at your organization's culture (see Chapter 2), you need to examine your own leadership approach.

Remember, when you curate or establish a mission and vision (the key components of culture), then any strategy in alignment with those can be planned and executed. Of course, this doesn't mean it will be all rainbows and butterflies from there.

As a leader, you have to be prepared to accept that not everyone will be on board. I've seen plenty of leaders exhaust their time and energy trying to convince a small group of employees to comply with strategic initiatives they don't agree with. Putting this kind of energy into changing minds is often a losing battle.

Not only are you unlikely to succeed, but you send a message to those who want to comply that you are focused on the negative. This can really impact morale and not in a good way. It's important for you as a leader to be okay with people, who aren't on board with the mission and vision, organically leaving the organization. This is not a failure of yours as a leader, but you may be letting others down if you don't right-size this situation.

HOW'S THAT WORKING FOR YOU?

I ask this question without judgment but with purposeful directness. If your team is thriving, your results are consistent, and your people are growing, your approach may be working well. But if you're experiencing turnover, missing targets, or feeling constant resistance, it's time for honest reflection.

Consider these questions:

- Do people seek your input or avoid interacting with you?
- Are you hearing honest concerns or just what people think you want to hear?
- Do you know what motivates each of your direct reports?

- When was the last time you admitted a mistake to your team?
- How do people respond when you enter a room?

WHAT'S YOUR LEADERSHIP STYLE?

Understanding your natural leadership style helps you leverage strengths and address blind spots. While there are many leadership frameworks, I find most leaders fall somewhere along these continuums:

Tell vs. Ask

- Do you provide clear directives or foster collaborative decision-making?
- When is each approach most effective in your organization?

Task-Focused vs. People-Focused

- Do you prioritize getting things done or building relationships?
- How does this affect team cohesion and performance?

Play It Safe vs. Take the Leap

- Do you encourage bold moves or careful, proven approaches?
- How does this shape innovation in your organization?

Straight Talk vs. Sugar-Coating

- Do you deliver unfiltered criticism or cushion difficult messages?
- How does your approach impact psychological safety?

None of these styles is inherently better or worse than others. It's human nature to lead based on how you've been conditioned and what has worked for you in the past. The key is applying the right approach for the situation and being adaptable. Adaptability is a huge part of leadership because one of your main jobs as a leader is to witness and manage constant change.

ARE YOU READY TO CHANGE?

This is the million-dollar question. Assessing culture and leadership is pointless if you are not prepared to change. Remember to give yourself grace. This is a marathon, not a sprint. There is no need to put pressure on yourself or to have all of this figured out by tomorrow. Your goal should be continuous learning. Make this your relentless pursuit and a lot of your biggest challenges will fade away.

I get it! Change is uncomfortable, especially for successful leaders. You've achieved results with your current approach. Your identity may be tied to certain leadership qualities. Shifting may feel like admitting failure rather than evolution. And there are unknowns with every change initiative.

 **TRUTH BOMB**

Here's what I know after two decades of coaching executives: The leaders who have the greatest impact are those willing to adapt their approach to serve their people and purpose, not those who force their people to adapt to their preferred leadership style.

One manufacturing CEO I coached, we'll call him Rick built his career on directive leadership—tell people what to do, and they'll do it. It worked for years until it didn't. A younger generation of employees wanted context, involvement, and meaning. Rather than dismissing this as "entitlement" and rolling his eyes at "kids today," he committed to evolving his approach. It wasn't easy, but it transformed his effectiveness.

Since I knew he preferred directness, I asked Rick a very direct question: "Bottom line, what do you want to get from your team members?" His answer: "I want them to deliver high performance." I told him he needed to focus on the "what" vs the "how."

We'll talk more specifically about bridging generational gaps below, but it's important to note here that Rick's biggest challenge was not his directness. Millennials and Gen Z workers in particular respond well to direct and explicit communication. It's just that Rick couldn't assume that his younger team members would simply do what he told them to do. He couldn't get high performance simply by asking for things like a two-page report summarizing client engagement trends.

Rick succeeded with a different approach. By showing them the desired result (e.g., showing them what a good report looks like), confirming understanding immediately, and checking in with them for alignment, Rick got what he wanted. Because he was willing to look at his own leadership and make a change, Rick was able to create a healthier culture for his team.

Ask yourself: What aspects of my leadership am I willing to examine and potentially change to create the culture my organization needs?

Addressing Modern Workplace Challenges

No, it's not your imagination. Today's workplace presents unique challenges that didn't exist a decade ago. Let's address some of the most pressing challenges I hear from leaders.

THE SOCIAL ISOLATION EPIDEMIC

"I find myself avoiding in-person meetings whenever possible."

"I'm just more comfortable behind a screen now."

"I dread social interactions that used to energize me."

These sentiments, once rare, now surface regularly in my coaching sessions—not just from introverts but from previously gregarious leaders. Post-pandemic, many experience a form of social atrophy that impacts their leadership effectiveness.

One senior vice president confided: "I used to walk the floor daily and knew everyone's name. Now I find myself staying in my office, sending emails instead of having conversations. I know it's hurting my team, but I can't seem to break the pattern."

This social withdrawal affects organizational culture profoundly. When leaders retreat behind digital walls, informal communication suffers, relationships weaken, and culture becomes amorphous.

The solution isn't forcing yourself into uncomfortable social marathons. Instead:

1. Start with brief, purposeful in-person interactions.
2. Schedule "walking meetings" with one or two people.
3. Create informal rituals that bring people together naturally.
4. Acknowledge the challenge openly — you're not alone.
5. Gradually expand your comfort zone through consistent practice.

Remember: Communication habits are like muscles; they atrophy without use but strengthen with consistent exercise.

THE MOTIVATION BALANCING ACT

Leaders today face a shaky balance: how to drive high performance without being perceived as authoritarian or insensitive.

A financial services executive recently told me: "I feel paralyzed. If I push too hard for results, I'm seen as uncaring. If I focus too much on people's well-being, our performance suffers. I can't win."

This tension is real, but the framing creates a false choice. The most effective leaders don't choose between results and relationships; they integrate them through:

Clarity about expectations: People want to know what success looks like. Vague standards create anxiety, not freedom.

Context about why the work matters: When people understand purpose, metrics become meaningful, not merely mechanical.

Consistency in approach: Unpredictable leadership creates walking-on-eggshells cultures where energy goes to figuring you out rather than doing great work.

Curiosity about constraints: Ask "What's getting in your way?" before assuming performance challenges reflect effort or ability.

> 💣 **TRUTH BOMB**
>
> The key is for you to communicate in a way that connects performance to purpose rather than compliance to command.

NAVIGATING BOUNDARIES AND AUTHENTICITY

"I'm afraid to be myself at work."

"I don't know what's appropriate to say anymore."

"Everything feels like a potential landmine."

These concerns cross generational and hierarchical lines, reflecting genuine uncertainty about workplace norms.

Leaders struggle with finding the balance between authenticity and appropriateness. Many lean more toward the side of caution, becoming so filtered they appear fake. Others resist changing long-established communication patterns, creating friction.

Neither extreme serves culture well. Instead, practice:

Intentional authenticity: Being authentic doesn't mean sharing every thought or feeling. It means ensuring your words align with your values and being transparent about your thinking when appropriate.

Curious learning: When norms shift, approach changes with curiosity rather than resistance. Ask: "Can you help me understand why this matters?" or "What is the desired outcome?" rather than dismissing new expectations.

Focusing on impact: Intention matters less than impact. If your communication style consistently creates unintended negative effects, adaptation is necessary to increase effectiveness.

Remember: Boundaries are guidelines that help us connect more effectively across differences. Contrary to popular belief, they aren't barriers to communication.

BRIDGING GENERATIONAL DIVIDES

Perhaps no area creates more communication challenges than generational differences. I often hear executives lament:

"These new graduates want to change everything before they understand how things work."

"The older managers won't adapt to the new communication tools we need."

While generational stereotypes are often overblown, different workplace experiences create real differences in communication expectations.

In Chapter 6, I'll discuss how to break down generational barriers. Here I want you to reflect on how you see people of different generations from your own. If you're a young career professional, do you look at the senior people who are old enough to be your parents and think, "They're totally out of touch" or "Why do they focus so much on details that don't matter?" If you're a senior leader and have been steeped in your industry for 20 or 30 years, do you look at the younger generation of professionals and think "When I started my career, no one was there to coddle me" or "What do these young people know about earning their place in this profession?"

If you've ever thought "Back in my day..." or "When I started my career, I didn't have this luxury..." or "Must be nice..." you might be harboring some resentment that could be expressed in passive aggressive ways. It's time to own those feelings instead of sweeping them under the rug.

A wise person once said something to me that was one of the biggest truth bombs I've personally embraced: "Stop expecting you from others." Generational differences often come down to a difference in boundaries; more accurately, one group expecting another to embrace the same boundaries. Those from older generations may struggle with seeing young people set and maintain boundaries because they feel powerless to create their own. They may think, "How dare you expect this boundary (e.g., work starting and ending at specific times, being able to work from home two or three days per week, being referred to by your preferred pronouns) to be respected when I didn't when I was in your position?" It's easy for all of us to default to thinking everyone experiences the world in the same way we do. When we are met with evidence disproving this assumption, it can be jarring. We fear what we don't understand.

>  **TRUTH BOMB**
>
> Stop expecting you from others.

Recognize that I'm not trying to place blame on anyone. I'm simply asking you to look at why you might have a reaction to someone from a different generation being bold enough to ask for what they need. I'm inviting you to use your power of communication to ask questions that will help you better understand, alleviate the resentment, and embrace others embracing their boundaries. For example, did you know that the younger generation (i.e., kids growing up in the early- and mid-2000s) watched their parents get burned out working 80 hours per week? They felt the impact of that in their families and they took note. With this perspective, it's easier to see why they would be so insistent about setting boundaries and unafraid to change jobs when they feel their boundaries are not being respected.

Rather than expecting conformity, address specific friction points:

Communication medium preferences: Establish clear guidelines about which channels are appropriate for different types of communication rather than letting each generation default to their preference. But remember, instead of taking a top-down approach, have a conversation with the whole team and talk about why you're making the decisions you're making.

Communication rhythm and approach: Create systems that support different communication preferences (e.g., regular check-ins for those who thrive on ongoing dialogue and structured reviews for those who prefer more formal, consolidated input).

Knowledge transfer mechanisms: Create intentional mentoring and reverse mentoring programs that value both experience and fresh perspective.

Work mode flexibility: Focus on outcomes rather than methods, allowing for different approaches while maintaining accountability. Give employees more agency over their work hours if their work can be done asynchronously.

The key is creating space for dialogue about these differences rather than letting frustration build through unexamined assumptions.

Effective Communication and Leadership Scenarios + Reflection (Assessment) Questions

INTRODUCTION

Listed below are some common real-world workplace scenarios. Each scenario provides an opportunity to practice identifying effective communication strategies and leadership practices that foster clarity, trust, and performance. Use this section to reflect on what you have learned, role-play different situations, and document takeaways for your leadership journey.

SECTION 1: CHALLENGING CONVERSATIONS

It's important to enter challenging conversations with the mindset of asking: "What support does this person need in order to navigate this challenge?"

Scenario 1: Delivering Applicable And Forward-Focused Input

Problem/Scenario: A high-performing employee's recent drop in performance is affecting team outcomes.

Solution: Prepare a private, specific, and supportive conversation that focuses on the behavior, its impact, and a collaborative plan for improvement.

Reflection Notes:

- What assessment tools and/or frameworks do you use?
- What tone and setting can you utilize to influence openness?

Scenario 2: Addressing Conflict Between Team Members

Ask: "Is this conflict bigger than our mission?"

Problem/Scenario: Ongoing tension between two team members is disrupting morale.

Solution: Facilitate a neutral mediation session with open dialogue, active listening, and mutual agreements.

Reflection Notes:

- What signals suggest unresolved conflict?
- How do you stay neutral as a leader?

Scenario 3: Correcting Miscommunication

Problem/Scenario: A project delay occurred due to unclear instructions.

Solution: Clarify objectives and responsibilities, and implement structured communication going forward.

Reflection Notes:

- Where can you improve clarity in your current communication?
- What tools/channels support this?

SECTION 2: TEAM COLLABORATION AND ENGAGEMENT

Scenario 4: Leading Cross-Functional Teams

Problem/Scenario: Departments with conflicting goals struggle to collaborate.

Solution: Align through a shared vision, common metrics, and inclusive forums.

Reflection Notes:

- How do you balance competing priorities?
- How is success defined across departments?

Scenario 5: Managing Remote Or Hybrid Teams

Problem/Scenario: Remote employees feel disconnected.

Solution: Level-set what engagement and visibility look and feel like for both remote and on-site team members, set norms, and ensure equal participation.

Reflection Notes:

- How do you maintain visibility and engagement?
- What check-ins are most effective?

Scenario 6: Building Psychological Safety

Problem/Scenario: Employees hesitate to speak up.

Solution: Model vulnerability, affirm contributions, and normalize curiosity.

Reflection Notes:

- What signals psychological safety?
- How do you respond to ideas you disagree with?

SECTION 3: ORGANIZATIONAL COMMUNICATION

Scenario 7: Communicating Change

Problem/Scenario: Employees show resistance to a major change due to fear/uncertainty.

Solution: Use transparent, empathetic messaging and invite input.

Reflection Notes:

- What's the story behind the change?
- How do you measure buy-in?

Scenario 8: Launching A New Vision Or Strategy

Problem/Scenario: Employees are unclear about a new direction.

Solution: Reinforce vision through storytelling and consistent messaging.

Reflection Notes:

- How do you make the vision real for your team?
- What language inspires action?

Scenario 9: Crisis Communication

Problem/Scenario: A crisis requires immediate clarity and direction.

Solution: Communicate swiftly, empathetically, and with accountability.

Reflection Notes:

- What's your role in a crisis?
- How do you balance urgency and calm?

SECTION 4: PERFORMANCE AND GOAL SETTING

Scenario 10: Conducting Effective One-on-Ones

Problem/Scenario: Employees feel unsupported.

Solution: Use one-on-ones to support growth, discuss progress, and check in on well-being.

Reflection Notes:

- What makes a one-on-one valuable?
- How do you track progress?

Scenario 11: Clarifying Roles and Responsibilities

Problem/Scenario: Ambiguous roles lead to inefficiencies.

Solution: Define roles using tools like RACI (Responsible, Accountable, Consulted, and Informed) and ensure alignment.[36]

Reflection Notes:

- Where do overlaps exist on your team?
- How is ownership communicated?

Scenario 12: Setting Smart Goals

Problem/Scenario: Team members are unclear about priorities.

Solution: Co-create SMART goals linked to business objectives.

Reflection Notes:

- Are your goals SMART?
- How are goals tracked and celebrated?

---

[36] Dana Miranda and Brett Day, "What is a RACI Chart? How this Project Management Tool Can Boost Your Productivity," *Forbes*, June 2, 2025 (https://www.forbes.com/advisor/business/raci-chart/).

SECTION 5: LEADERSHIP PRESENCE AND INFLUENCE

Scenario 13: Leading Without Authority

Problem/Scenario: You must influence others without formal power.

Solution: Build relationships, use data, and align asks with shared goals.

Reflection Notes:

- What builds credibility and trust?
- How do you position your message?

Scenario 14: Executive Communication

Problem/Scenario: You have difficulty presenting to senior leadership.

Solution: Use structured frameworks, keep messaging concise, and anticipate questions.

Reflection Notes:

- How do you adapt for executive audiences?
- Can you explain your core message in two minutes?

Scenario 15: Onboarding New Leaders or Team Members

Problem/Scenario: New hires feel disconnected and overwhelmed.

Solution: Create a structured, relational onboarding experience.

Reflection Notes:

- What does a successful first 30 days look like?
- How do you introduce culture and norms?

FINAL REFLECTION

- Which scenario feels most relevant to your current role?
- What new strategy or insight will you apply this month?

Looking Forward

Culture assessment is an ongoing practice of observation, reflection, and adjustment. The most effective leaders I've worked with maintain a beginner's mind, constantly questioning their assumptions about what's happening in their organizations and with their teams.

As you reflect on your culture and leadership, remember that meaningful change doesn't require wholesale transformation. Small, consistent shifts in how you communicate can dramatically impact how people experience your culture.

In the next chapter, we'll explore how to move toward creating a culture of belonging through the three pillars of transparency, vulnerability, and humanity and how these elements form the foundation for truly inclusive organizations where everyone can thrive.

Chapter 6
Moving in the Right Direction

> "Stay away from people who act like a victim in a problem they created."
>
> –Dr. Dale C. Bronner, bishop, author, and leadership trainer

The difference between a workplace where people merely show up and a workplace where people thrive comes down to one word: belonging. When people feel they belong, they bring their full capabilities, creativity, and commitment. When they don't, they bring compliance at best, and often that compliance is begrudging.

I've worked with organizations across the spectrum — from those where people count the minutes until they can leave to those where people feel so connected to the mission and each other that the lines between work and passion blur. The difference isn't benefits, compensation, or even the work itself. It's whether people feel truly seen, valued, and connected.

Creating this sense of belonging isn't accidental. It's intentional, consistent work built on three foundational pillars: transparency, vulnerability, and humanity.

Why Real Talk Wins: The C-Suite's Secret Sauce for Leading with Transparency, Vulnerability, and Humanity

PILLAR 1: TRANSPARENCY — TRUST IS THE REAL FLEX

People follow leaders they believe in, and nothing builds belief like honesty and transparency. Show up real, and your people will show up for you. Every time.

But what is transparency? Transparency means sharing not just what decisions are made, but how and why they're made. It means providing context, admitting limitations, and being forthright about challenges. Employees are more likely to trust leaders who are open about challenges, decisions, and emotions. And from a business perspective, trust boosts morale and reduces turnover, which promotes institutional knowledge and team cohesion.

When I worked with a manufacturing company undergoing significant restructuring, the CEO initially wanted to shield employees from the full financial reality. "I don't want to create panic," he told me. Although his instinct to shield his employees was coming from good intentions — he wasn't trying to withhold information — the vacuum of information created something worse: rumors, speculation, and distrust.

We shifted the approach. The CEO told me he had an all-hands meeting coming up. It was the perfect opportunity for him to practice being more transparent. We agreed that he would share specific financial challenges, the options considered, and the reasoning behind the difficult decisions. He would also outline what was known, what remained uncertain, and the principles guiding the company's choices. I worked with him to plan his remarks.

First, I insisted that he not use a script. His initial reaction was "no way." I needed to explain my reasoning. Here it is: Many CEOs develop a formal dependency on their communications team. While I respect that you're representing the company, speaking without the help of a script allows you to connect with your audience on a personal level. Speaking from a script written by someone else (or even a script you write) creates a wall between you and the people who need to hear your message. Your employees can sense when you're reading corporate-speak versus when you're speaking from the heart. They want to hear *you* — your conviction, your humanity, your genuine concern for their future. That kind of transparency can't be captured in pre-written talking points. Instead, feel free to write down some talking points, and allow yourself to speak from the heart.

I took him through the following simple exercise:

> **THE TWO-COLUMN CLARITY EXERCISE**
>
> **Step 1:** Take a sheet of paper and make two columns.
>
> **Step 2:** On the left side, write down your core values and how you apply them as a leader.
>
> **Step 3:** On the right side, write down others' feelings and values (e.g., mental health, keeping their job).
>
> **Step 4:** Consider the two columns together to help you decide what you want to say.

The goal was finding a way to be transparent without sugar-coating the situation or putting the company at unnecessary risk. I coached him to tell people directly: "This is difficult." I told him, as I tell all leaders, "Don't place blame. Take ownership. Talk to your audience like you're talking to me in this room right now. Clarity is your power as a leader."

When you need to have a difficult conversation with your employees, think about it like being a parent. If you don't talk to your kids about important topics like sex, they'll find information elsewhere, and it might not be accurate or what you want them to hear. People don't know what they don't know. So clearly state what you do know:

revenue has dropped, costs have increased, funding has been delayed. It's okay to talk about these realities. Then clearly state what you intend to do and why.

> **TRUTH BOMB**
>
> The truth hurts... one time. There's a saying that the truth hurts. And it's accurate. However, as a leader, you need to understand that the truth hurts once, while lies or redirection hurt over and over. When you're honest upfront, it creates ripples of shared responsibility, honesty, and trust.

After the all-hands meeting, the CEO and I debriefed. He told me something interesting. At first, the room went completely silent and he panicked, thinking he'd said the wrong thing. But then he realized they weren't silent because they were afraid to say anything. They were silent because they were listening. Really listening. The senior leadership team noticed it too. That moment of vulnerability allowed his employees to move into a circle of shared trust, responsibility, and honesty.

The response surprised him. Rather than panic, employees appreciated being treated as partners in the solution. Several even came forward with cost-saving ideas that hadn't been considered.

Of course, transparency doesn't mean sharing everything. It doesn't mean opening up your books to your employees. It doesn't mean burdening your frontline workers with inappropriate emotions.

> **TRUTH BOMB**
>
> Transparency means sharing what matters in ways that empower rather than overwhelm.

Leaders, consider these practices:

Decision transparency: Explain not just decisions but decision-making processes. What factors were considered? What alternatives were explored?

No one likes mystery meetings or vague memos. Clear, open communication keeps your culture fresh, focused, and thriving. If this feels challenging, remind yourself that letting people in means more brains in the game. You get better ideas, fewer blind spots, and waaaaay less cleanup later.

Financial transparency: Help people understand the business realities that drive priorities. When people understand how money flows through the organization, they make better day-to-day decisions.

When the boss keeps it real, the team steps up too. Transparency sets the tone for owning mistakes and sharing wins. Public commitments or transparent reflections from the top model accountability, which encourages the same from middle management and frontline staff.

Again, effective transparency is about sharing what people need to know to succeed, not revealing every internal detail.

Change transparency: During times of change, share what you know, what you don't know, and when you expect to know more. Regular updates, even when there's little new information, keep the trust flowing during times of uncertainty.

Open leaders calm the chaos. They name the hard stuff and lead through it. Transparency asks us to remember that people follow confidence, not perfection.

>  **TIME OUT**
>
> One caution about transparency: timing matters. Sharing half-formed ideas prematurely can create unnecessary anxiety. Avoid sharing simply to relieve your own anxiety. You have to be strong for your people and share when it's appropriate. Yet this caution often becomes an excuse for permanent opacity, rooted in how we were conditioned to view vulnerability as weakness.
>
> We've all lived through a pandemic that fundamentally shifted how we connect and show up in the workplace. The pandemic shattered many of these old assumptions about workplace transparency. Suddenly, leaders who had always projected unwavering confidence found themselves saying things like, "We don't know what's going to happen" and "We're figuring this out as we go." And you know what? Instead of losing credibility, many of these leaders actually strengthened their relationships with their teams. Employees appreciated the honesty about uncertainty rather than false reassurances that everything was under control.
>
> The pandemic taught us that people can handle difficult truths better than we often assume. They'd rather know that leadership is actively navigating challenges than be left in the dark, wondering what's really happening. The leaders who thrived during this period weren't those who had all the answers — they were those who could communicate honestly about what they knew, what they didn't know, and what they were doing to find solutions.

A Deeper Picture: The Leadership Cost of Withheld Truths

Imagine this: You're sitting in a meeting when you hear a major update, one that directly impacts your role, your team, or a decision you made just days ago. But here's the thing: it's not new information to everyone. You quickly realize others knew well before you. You, though, have had no warning. No heads-up. No opportunity to prepare or weigh in.

What's your first thought? "If you had just been upfront with me from the beginning…"

It's not the news itself that stings. It's the delay. The secrecy. The erosion of trust that happens in silence.

We all understand companies and leaders evolve. Decisions shift. Not everything is final at first. However, being left out of the loop, especially when your work or reputation is on the line, doesn't just feel like an oversight. It feels like a betrayal. It signals that your input wasn't valued or that your superiors didn't trust your ability to handle the truth.

Here's the hard truth about leadership:

People don't expect you to have all the answers. They don't expect you to be perfect. What they do expect is honesty. They respect a leader who can say, "Here's what we know. Here's what we don't. And here's what we're working through." That kind of clarity is grounding. It gives people something to stand on, even if the ground is still shifting.

When you withhold information under the banner of "we're still figuring it out," but never return with updates, you're unintentionally excluding people from the process. That absence of communication breeds suspicion.

The most respected leaders understand that their team's trust isn't built on perfect news, but on consistent honesty. Think about Jimmy Carter who, during his 1976 campaign, made the bold promise: "I will always tell you the truth, even when it's not great news." This guiding principle created a lifelong legacy that extended far beyond his presidency. The impact of his transparency and vulnerability transcended politics, ultimately leading to his Nobel Prize.

 **TRUTH BOMB**

Transparency is not a luxury; it's a responsibility.

True leadership reveals itself not just on sunny days, but in the midst of the storm. When it's uncomfortable... when the stakes are high... when the news is not what people want to hear but what they need to hear... and when it's shared with intentionality, respect, and humanity... it builds something far more powerful than short-term harmony. It builds trust.

PILLAR #2: VULNERABILITY — THE COURAGE TO BE SEEN

At this point, I could tell you what leadership isn't about. However, I'd rather tell you what leadership is. You ready? Let's go.

Leadership is about creating the conditions where collective intelligence can emerge. People sometimes make the mistake of believing leadership is about being understood. In reality, it's much more about seeking to understand. You can honor your experience while making space for theirs.

And this requires vulnerability. Vulnerability in leadership is the courage to be seen as fully human. It means acknowledging mistakes, admitting uncertainty, and showing genuine emotion when appropriate.

 TIME OUT

I get it. As soon as you see that word "vulnerability," I know you have reservations. What I'm asking you to do requires courage because it can be very difficult at times. However, it's necessary in creating a culture of trust.

Based on my experience, I realize being open about uncertainties or mistakes can feel risky, especially when people are looking to you for direction. There's an expectation to always have it together. And that pressure makes it hard to admit when we don't have all the answers.

> Many of us were taught that strong leadership means showing confidence at all times. However, if we focus on creating that culture of trust, we discover that vulnerability actually enhances rather than undermines our authority.

One of my clients, a senior executive at a financial services firm, built her career on projecting unwavering confidence. "If I show any doubt, my team will lose confidence in me," she insisted. But her team was already disengaging precisely because her polished facade felt like a front and created impossible standards.

I encouraged her to try a more vulnerable approach, while still maintaining her confident demeanor. During a strategy session that wasn't producing results, she took a deep breath and said, "I need to be honest. I don't have the answer here, and I'm feeling stuck. I need your help."

The energy in the room transformed instantly. Team members who had been silent became engaged. Ideas flowed. The problem wasn't solved immediately, but the relationship between the leader and team fundamentally shifted.

Vulnerability practices that strengthen belonging include:

Acknowledging mistakes: "I made the wrong call on that project" is far more powerful than "the project faced unexpected challenges."

Sharing learning journeys: When leaders talk about their own growth areas and learning edges, they create permission for others to develop without shame. And while it's good to share learning journeys after the fact, it's even better to share when you're in the messy middle of a challenge.

Asking for help: Demonstrating that you don't have all the answers and genuinely need others' expertise creates investment and ownership.

Showing appropriate emotion: Expressing authentic feelings, whether excitement about a new opportunity or disappointment about a setback, humanizes leadership.

When leaders get real, teams follow suit — and that's when the magic starts. Bold ideas? Flying. Honest conversations? Flowing. Creative sparks? Everywhere. Vulnerability is an invitation. When leaders go first, they crack open space for open dialogue, brave thinking, and the kind of honesty that actually gets stuff done.

Teams feel safer taking calculated risks and speaking up, which is essential for growth and progress.

The key word in all of this is "appropriate." Vulnerability means authentic expression that serves the relationship and the work. That's very different from emotional dumping or shifting your emotional processing onto your team.

PILLAR #3: HUMANITY — SEEING THE WHOLE PERSON

Humanity means recognizing that people are never just their job functions. They bring their full selves — their histories, identities, challenges, and aspirations — to work every day.

At a healthcare organization I worked with, a new director was struggling to connect with her team. On paper, she was doing everything right: setting clear expectations, holding regular check-ins, offering development opportunities. But something was missing.

During one of our coaching sessions, she realized she knew almost nothing about her team members as people (e.g., their backgrounds, their motivations, what mattered to them outside work). She'd been so focused on operational excellence that she'd missed the human connection.

She began integrating simple practices — taking a genuine interest in people's lives, remembering personal details, creating space for connection before diving into work topics. Within months, team cohesion and performance improved dramatically.

Humanity practices include:

Meaningful check-ins: Start meetings with brief questions that allow people to share something beyond their task list. "What's a win you had this week — work or personal?" creates space for whole-person recognition. It's okay if it feels a little forced at first. The intention matters and it will shine through if you use this in addition to other practices.

Life accommodation: Recognize that people have responsibilities and challenges outside work. When leaders accommodate reality rather than pretending it doesn't exist, people bring more energy and focus when they are working.

Celebration and recognition: Mark both professional milestones and personal ones. Simple acknowledgments of life events signal that you see the whole person.

Cultural humility: Learn about the diverse backgrounds, traditions, and perspectives people bring, recognizing that your experience isn't universal.

One leader I worked with initially dismissed these practices as "soft" and unnecessary. Six months later, after implementing them with his team, he told me: "I used to think my job was getting results from people. Now I understand my job is creating the conditions where people deliver exceptional results because they want to." That's a perfect reframe.

Today's talent wants leaders who are bold and human. If you're not being real, you're being replaced. Today's workforce, especially Gen Z and Millennials, expects honesty, emotional intelligence, and authenticity from leaders. Vulnerable leadership isn't a trend — it's a requirement in the modern workplace.

> **SELF-TALK: YOUR INNER COMMUNICATION COACH**
>
> I'm a big advocate of positive self-talk. Here are some phrases you can use as part of your efforts to become more vulnerable and transparent:
>
> - "I'm working on being more open, even when the path forward isn't crystal clear."
> - "This may feel like a vulnerable share, but I believe it's important to be real."
> - "I've held back in the past out of fear it would cause doubt. I realize now that clarity and honesty build more trust than silence ever will."
> - "I used to think that transparency and vulnerability were inherently weak. I now know they're one of the most powerful tools for connection."
>
> Write them on sticky notes and paste them on your mirror and say them out loud as you get ready in the morning.

Building Inclusive Communication Systems

Leaders behaving in alignment with these three pillars is a good start, but belonging also requires systems that enable everyone to contribute their perspectives and capabilities. These systems must be intentionally designed to overcome the natural tendencies toward exclusion that exist in most organizations.

FROM SELECTIVE HEARING TO ACTIVE LISTENING

In too many organizations, who gets heard depends on factors unrelated to the value of their contribution. This includes factors like their position, how they look, how well they've been trained to "play the game," and whether they share communication preferences with those in power.

A technology company I consulted with faced persistent problems with product launches. Despite extensive testing, their products consistently missed users' critical needs. The breakthrough came when we mapped their decision-making process and realized they were hearing from only a narrow segment of voices, primarily senior engineers who shared similar backgrounds and thinking styles.

We implemented structured listening processes that specifically sought out perspectives from:

- Customer-facing roles who got firsthand reactions from customers.
- Team members with diverse backgrounds.
- Newer employees without the "we've always done it this way" filter.
- Those with stronger listening skills and introverted styles.

The impact was immediate. Their next product launch addressed user needs more comprehensively and required fewer post-launch fixes.

Inclusive listening systems include:

Multiple input channels: Some people speak up in meetings; others prefer writing; others share thoughts one on one. Multiple channels ensure you hear from everyone, not just those comfortable with dominant communication modes.

Structured turn-taking: Simple practices like round-robins or ensuring everyone speaks before anyone speaks twice can transform participation patterns.

Divergence before convergence: Creating space for all ideas before evaluation prevents early momentum from silencing alternative perspectives.

Listening systems: Regular, anonymous ways for people to share concerns creates safety for raising challenges that might otherwise remain hidden.

The key here is to recognize that there's a lot of power in being a listener more than a talker. In fact, the need for active listening, especially now when customers have higher expectations of the companies they buy from, is just as critical as the need for people with extroverted styles.

FROM INFORMATION PRIVILEGE TO INFORMATION EQUITY

In most organizations, information access correlates with position power. Those higher in the hierarchy receive more context, earlier updates, and greater insight into decision-making. This creates tiered citizenship where some operate with full information while others make decisions in a partial vacuum.

One retail organization I worked with struggled with store-level execution until they realized their frontline managers were making decisions without critical context available to corporate leaders. Think about it like making a strawberry shortcake pie (those who know me know that I LOVE to eat!). You need all the right ingredients and tools to create something delicious. Their managers were trying to bake without knowing what was in the pantry! These frontline leaders had the flour and sugar (basic operational guidelines), but were missing the strawberries and cream (strategic context) that would make everything come together.

When executives recognized this gap, they realized it was "time to go back into the kitchen" and reassess their recipe for success. By creating information equity, ensuring key strategic context reached all decision-makers regardless of level, they improved both execution and engagement. Just as a missing ingredient might still produce an edible but unsatisfying dessert, these stores were functioning but not thriving. Once all team members had access to the complete recipe, the whole organization could deliver something truly excellent. For you scientists out there, it was like going back into the lab to ensure everyone had the complete formula, not just parts of the equation.

Information equity practices include:

Context cascades: Ensure key strategic context — the "why" behind decisions — reaches every level, not just action items.

Accessible language: Eliminate insider jargon and acronyms that create invisible barriers to understanding.

Information transparency: Make information accessible by default rather than restricted by default, limiting only what truly requires confidentiality.

Decision visibility: Make clear how decisions are made and who makes them so people know where to direct input.

FROM CONFORMITY PRESSURE TO IDENTITY SAFETY

As we saw in Chapter 3, belonging doesn't mean fitting in. It means being valued for your distinctive contributions. Many organizations undermine belonging by creating subtle pressures to conform to dominant norms in communication style, work approach, or personal presentation.

A consulting firm I worked with couldn't understand why they struggled to retain women and people of color despite recruiting diverse talent. Through culture interviews, we discovered an unspoken expectation that "successful consultants" exhibited a specific communication style (assertive, quick to speak, and comfortable with debate-style interactions).

This created a constant adaptation tax on anyone whose natural style differed from this norm. They were essentially doing two jobs: their actual work and the exhausting work of conforming to communication expectations that didn't align with their strengths.

We worked with them to expand their definition of effective communication to recognize multiple styles. All of these styles are important voices to have at the table.

The Slow Jam Thinker: Gives things a beat to breathe. Processes deeply and brings big-picture, meaningful insights to the table when everyone else is still reacting. Their thoughts are like fine wine, worth the wait.

> **Vibe:** *They don't rush the mic — they vibe, reflect, and drop wisdom when it really matters.*

The Idea DJ: This person builds bridges between brainstorms. They make connections others miss and turn half-formed ideas into full-on brilliance. Always team-first, always thinking in "we."

> **Vibe:** *Takes your idea, spins it with someone else's, and creates a remix that slaps.*

The Provocateur: Not here for small talk, they're here to dig deeper. They light up the room with curiosity, asking questions that spark clarity, creativity, and better decisions.

> **Vibe:** *Ask 'em one question, and they'll ask you five that make you rethink your whole plan — in the best way.*

The Clarity Captain: While others get lost in the weeds, this person zooms out, listens in, and boils it all down to what really matters. They make sense out of mess and bring next steps into focus.

> **Vibe:** *Turns the chaos into calm, and makes you say, "Ahhh, now I get it."*

By explicitly valuing these different approaches, they reduced conformity pressure and increased retention of diverse talent. When you work to develop inclusive communication systems, employees feel safe to bring their whole selves to work. In other words, you're creating identity safety.

TIME OUT

Hold up. Identity safety? What's that? You are likely familiar with the term psychological safety, which is about creating an environment where people feel secure to contribute fully, challenge the status quo, and be vulnerable, knowing that their input will be respected and valued.

As I've mentioned throughout this book, psychological safety is foundational for high-performing teams, fostering open communication, innovation, and collaboration.[37]

---

[37] Katrien Fransen, Desmond McEwan, and Mustafa Sarkar, "The impact of identity leadership on team functioning and well-being in team sport: Is psychological safety the missing link?" *Psychology of Sport and Exercise*, November 2020 (https://www.sciencedirect.com/science/article/abs/pii/S1469029220301497).

> Identity safety refers to the psychological state where individuals feel they can be their real selves in a workplace or social environment without facing negative consequences, judgment, or devaluation because of their personal identity characteristics (e.g., race, gender, sexual orientation, religion, or other aspects of identity).[38]
>
> It exists when people don't feel they need to downplay, hide, or modify aspects of their identity (such as race, gender, sexual orientation, religion, cultural background, or even personal communication style and work approach) to be accepted and valued. And it's just as valuable as psychological safety.

In an identity-safe environment:

- People can bring their whole selves to work without facing an "adaptation tax" for which they constantly monitor and adjust their natural behaviors.
- Different ways of thinking, communicating, and working are recognized as valuable rather than deficient.
- Contributions are evaluated on their merit rather than filtered through identity-based assumptions.
- Cultural differences are viewed as assets that enhance the organization rather than deviations from a preferred norm.
- Accommodations for different needs and approaches are normalized rather than treated as special exceptions.

Identity safety is distinct from mere tolerance or inclusion because it goes beyond allowing differences to actively valuing them as sources of strength and innovation.

---

38 Sacha Thompson, "The Intersection of Psychological Safety and Identity: Why It Matters Now More Than Ever," *DEI After 5*, November 19, 2024 (https://theequityequationllc.com/2024/11/19/psych_safety_and_identity).

Identity safety practices include:

Style flexibility: Create meetings and workflows that accommodate different working and communication styles rather than privileging one approach.

For example:

- Offer a mix of synchronous and asynchronous discussion options for team decisions.
- Provide meeting agendas in advance for those who process information better with preparation time.
- Implement "write first, then discuss" protocols that favor both reflective and spontaneous thinkers.
- Create dedicated quiet spaces for focused work alongside collaborative areas.
- Rotate meeting facilitation styles to accommodate different leadership approaches.
- Use digital tools with multiple participation options (e.g., chat, voice, polling).

Explicit values for inclusion: Move beyond vague commitments to specific, observable behaviors that demonstrate how inclusion works in practice.

For example:

- "We value diverse perspectives" becomes "In meetings, we ensure everyone speaks before anyone speaks twice."
- "We're committed to equity" becomes "We review compensation quarterly to identify and address disparities."
- "We honor diversity" becomes "We actively solicit and implement insights from underrepresented team members."
- Create a clear process for identifying exclusive practices.
- Establish clear metrics for measuring inclusion across teams and departments.
- Define observable leadership behaviors that model inclusive practices.

Normalized accommodation: Make accommodation the standard rather than the exception—whether it's flexible schedules, communication preferences, or work approaches.

For example:

- Implement core collaboration hours (e.g., 11am–3pm) while allowing flexibility outside those times.
- Create standard documentation practices that support information accessibility for all learning styles.
- Offer closed captioning as a default for all video meetings.
- Design all-team events with multiple participation options (i.e., in-person, remote, asynchronous).
- Build work processes that naturally accommodate diverse working styles.
- Create standardized but adjustable onboarding paths that adapt to individual learning preferences.

Cultural tradition recognition: Acknowledge and honor the diverse traditions, holidays, and practices people bring rather than defaulting to dominant cultural norms.

For example:

- Maintain a shared cultural calendar highlighting team members' important celebrations.
- Implement flexible PTO policies that accommodate diverse religious observances.
- Create food options at company events that respect various cultural and dietary preferences.
- Incorporate diverse cultural perspectives when developing products and services.
- Establish quiet spaces for prayer, meditation, or cultural practices.
- Celebrate heritage months authentically through employee-led education rather than superficial decorations.

Breaking Down Generational Barriers

In the previous chapter, I said few challenges create more communication friction than generational differences. While generational stereotypes are often overblown, different workplace experiences and historical contexts do create real differences in communication expectations and styles.

Leading younger generations often comes with a number of feelings, and being led by older generations also comes with a number of feelings. Both groups can experience judgment, resentment, frustration, and overall disconnect. Let's acknowledge these feelings, so we can reclaim the relationship.

It's okay to admit the feelings that you have when working with people in different generations. It's not okay to stay there. If you're the leader, you have to make the first move in repairing the trust that may have eroded. You can do this by leading with curiosity, not comparison.

Beyond Stereotypes: Understanding Generational Context

Rather than focusing on caricatures of generational differences, effective leaders understand the formative experiences that shape different generations' approaches to work and communication.

CONTRASTING GENERATIONAL EXPERIENCES

Older Generations:

- Built careers when information was scarce (pre-internet).
- Value depth of knowledge and expertise.
- Experienced one-way communication from supervisors.
- Were accustomed to managers who often lectured without inviting input from younger participants.

Younger Generations:

- Grew up with information abundance.
- Value finding, filtering, and applying diverse information.
- Benefit from shifts in leadership philosophy.
- Use digital tools (smartphones, Slack, Zoom) for instant communication.
- Expect voices to be heard.

Neither approach is inherently better, but without understanding the context, these differences can create friction.

BRIDGING THE GAP

Get curious about individual perspectives and consider how each group can get what they need.

- **For younger generations working with the old guard:** Consider what they need but might not know how to ask for. Many experienced professionals struggle with seeking or taking advice from younger colleagues.
- **For older generations:** Recognize that younger colleagues might have been trained not to question their elders.

Ask yourself: What would earn their respect?

SUCCESS STORY

One manufacturing company bridged this gap by creating cross-generational communities of practice around key skills. Rather than positioning it as experienced workers teaching newer ones, they framed it as an experience exchange:

- Veteran employees shared deep process knowledge.
- Newer employees shared digital workflow techniques.

This mutual value exchange created connection instead of competition.

USING EMPATHY MAPPING

Put yourself in the shoes of someone you don't understand or find yourself in conflict with, then map out:

- What might they feel frustrated about?
- What do they need that they wouldn't necessarily ask for?

What Is an Empathy Map?

An empathy map typically divides a person's experience into four quadrants:

1. **Thinking and Feeling:** What might the person be thinking? What matters to them? What worries or excites them?
2. **Seeing:** What does the person observe in their environment? What are they exposed to daily?
3. **Saying and Doing:** What might the person say or do publicly? How might they behave in observable ways?
4. **Hearing:** What messages is the person receiving from colleagues, friends, authority figures, and media?

Emotional Reframing Exercise:
From Resentment to Curiosity

If you feel resentment toward someone else, try this exercise developed by Dr. Gabor Mate.[39]

Step 1: Recall a Recent Frustration

Think of a recent moment when you felt upset, frustrated, or disappointed with someone. This could be something small or something more significant — just something you're open to reflecting on.

Step 2: Name What Happened

Briefly describe the situation. What happened factually? Who was involved? What was said or done?

Step 3: Identify Your Emotional Reaction

What did you feel in that moment? Try to name the core emotions (e.g., anger, sadness, frustration, shame, disappointment).

Step 4: Ask Yourself: What Did I Make It Mean?

What story did you tell yourself about why this happened? Did you assume the other person didn't care, didn't respect you, or thought you weren't important?

Step 5: Explore Other Possibilities

List at least three alternative reasons for the person's behavior that have nothing to do with you.

---

39 "Dr. Gabor Mate on How to Reframe a Challenging Moment and Feel Empowered," *The Tim Ferriss Show* (https://www.youtube.com/watch?v=__JLFw2FtEQ).

For example:

- They were overwhelmed or dealing with a personal crisis.
- They forgot or misunderstood what was needed.
- They struggle with follow-through or communication.

Step 6: Connect to the Pattern

Ask: *Have I felt this way before?*

Is this a familiar wound — perhaps from earlier in life — about feeling unimportant, disrespected, or unloved?

Step 7: Reclaim Your Power

Recognize that the emotional intensity might not just be about the present situation, but about a deeper belief you've carried. What might that belief be (e.g., "I'm not worthy of care," "People always let me down," "I have to do everything myself.")?

Now gently challenge it: What if that belief isn't true? What if you are fully worthy of care and respect?

Step 8: Reframe

Finish this sentence:

Instead of feeling resentment about [insert the situation or person], I'm choosing to get curious about [insert your deeper insight or alternative perspective].

Example:

Instead of feeling resentment about my contractor not finishing the job, I'm choosing to get curious about why I jumped to the conclusion that it meant I always put my trust in the wrong people.

LEVERAGING GENERATIONAL STRENGTHS

The most successful organizations move beyond accommodation to actively leveraging the different strengths generations bring.

1. Institutional Knowledge Capture

Prevent loss of crucial historical/contextual insight when long-tenured employees leave or retire.

Examples:

- **Legacy Interviews:** Conduct recorded video interviews with long-tenured employees where they share lessons learned, project histories, client anecdotes, and problem-solving insights. Organize clips into a searchable library.
- **"If I Leave Tomorrow" Docs:** Ask veteran staff to complete a short guide answering, "If I left tomorrow, here's what I'd want you to know..." covering processes, pitfalls, and tribal knowledge.
- **Internal Wiki with Annotations:** Build a collaborative wiki where experienced employees document workflows, decisions, and best practices — with the ability for others to comment or ask questions.
- **Knowledge Transfer Pods:** Pair senior employees with mid-level colleagues for 6–8 weeks to shadow and co-document workflows and nuanced decision-making processes.

2. Fresh Perspective Forums

Create space for newer employees to offer insights unfiltered by company habits or history.

Examples:

- **30/60/90-Day Insight Panels:** Invite new hires to a panel discussion after 30, 60, and 90 days to share what surprised them, what felt broken, and what ideas they have for improvement while their impressions are still fresh.
- **"Beginner's Mind" Roundtable:** Quarterly open forums where employees with <1 year tenure are invited to share ideas and

observations, facilitated by a leader who listens without defensiveness.
- **Flip the Town Hall:** Instead of executives talking, give the floor to new hires to present "What I'd do if I ran this department," encouraging bold thinking and surfacing blind spots.
- **Newbie-Led Audits:** Assign new employees to "audit" internal processes (like onboarding, project management, customer experience) and report inefficiencies or opportunities.

3. Cross-Generational Mentoring

Foster mutual learning between older and younger employees; value experience and innovation.

Examples:

- **Reverse Mentoring Program:** Pair junior employees with senior leaders, where the junior partner mentors the senior in areas like tech, social media, DEI, or new work trends while gaining valuable career guidance in return.
- **"Mentor Match Days":** Host speed-networking-style events where employees of different generations are matched for one-to-one conversations based on interests, not hierarchy.
- Generational Co-Labs: Set up cross-functional projects in which teams must include members from at least three different decades of age/experience to design solutions collaboratively.
- **Two-Way Storytelling Series:** Host informal monthly sessions where one senior and one junior employee tell stories about their work experience and lessons learned, followed by discussion.

4. Mixed-Experience Teams

Design teams that intentionally blend generations and experience levels to boost innovation, balance risk, and foster mutual respect.

Examples:

- **Innovation Sprints with Experience Quotas:** When forming short-term innovation or problem-solving teams, require

a mix of early-career, mid-career, and late-career team members to ensure diverse thinking styles and comfort zones are represented.
- **Cross-Gen Project Pods:** For major projects (e.g., system overhauls, culture change initiatives), build pods that include a Gen Z digital native, a Gen X or Boomer with legacy process knowledge, and someone mid-career to bridge perspectives.
- **Co-Leadership Models:** Assign co-leads from different career stages (e.g., a senior manager and an emerging leader) to encourage balanced decision-making and shared accountability.
- **Generational "Sherpas" for Change Initiatives:** Pair team members with different experience levels to navigate transitions (like adopting new tools or workflows), so tech-savvy employees help with digital adoption while veterans provide context on past pitfalls.

Fostering Psychological Safety Through Communication

Belonging requires psychological safety: the belief that you can speak up, offer ideas, admit mistakes, and ask questions without fear of punishment or humiliation. Similar to identity safety, psychological safety emerges primarily through consistent communication patterns.

FROM JUDGMENT TO CURIOSITY

The fastest way to shut down belonging is responding to contributions with judgment rather than curiosity. I worked with a technology executive who couldn't understand why his team rarely offered ideas in meetings. When I observed his typical response to suggestions (immediately pointing out flaws or limitations), the reason became clear.

We worked on shifting his default response from evaluation to exploration. Instead of "Here's why that won't work," he practiced "Tell me more about how you see that working." The change in team participation was dramatic.

Scripts: Practicing Curiosity

Curiosity practices include:

1. Asking Before Answering

When someone raises a concern or suggestion, ask questions before offering your perspective.

Examples:

- "That's an interesting point about our customer service approach. Could you share what led you to that observation?"
- "Before I respond to your suggestion about the project timeline, I'd like to understand. What specific challenges are you anticipating with our current schedule?"
- "You've raised concerns about our onboarding process. Can you tell me which parts you found most challenging and why?"
- "That's a different approach to our marketing strategy than we've considered. What outcomes do you think this might help us achieve?"
- "That's a creative idea for our client presentation. What aspects of the client's needs do you think this would address particularly well?"

2. Genuine Inquiry

Ask questions you don't know the answer to rather than using questions to lead people to your predetermined conclusion.

Examples:

- **Instead of:** "Don't you think we should go with option A?"
  Try: "What stands out to you about each of these options? What might we be missing?"
- **"Curiosity Circles":** During team discussions, designate a round where only genuine questions are allowed — no

solutions, no pitches, just open-ended curiosity like, "What would happen if...?" or "Why do you think this has been hard to solve?"

- **Leadership Practice:** In one-on-ones or reviews, ask "What's something you see that I might not?" or "What's been surprising or challenging in this project for you?" These questions signal you're here to learn, not just to steer.

- **Meeting Ground Rule:** "Ask at least one question today that you truly don't know the answer to." Then reflect afterward: what did you learn?

3. Exploration Before Evaluation

Create intangible space (e.g., it may even be in that moment, just giving them quiet and space to let their creative juices flow) to develop ideas before assessing them.

Examples:

- **Idea Incubation Time:** After someone presents an idea, pause for 2-5 minutes of quiet reflection or journaling before opening it up for discussion. It slows the rush to critique and honors the creative process.

- **"Yes, and..." Brainstorms:** For 10 minutes, only build on each other's ideas with "Yes, and..." responses — no "but" or critique allowed until a second phase.

- **The "Bubble" Technique:** Create protected space during ideation meetings where new thoughts are "in the bubble." They're allowed to be weird, unfinished, or rough without immediate analysis or ranking.

- **Solo Think Time in Meetings:** Before group ideation, give everyone 3 minutes to write down their own ideas privately. Then share without comment until all voices are heard. It reduces groupthink and gives introverts a fair shot.

4. Separating Ideas from Identity

Focus input and suggestions on specific ideas rather than making it about the person.

Examples:

- **Language Shift:** Use phrases like "This idea might benefit from…" instead of "You didn't consider…" Focus on the proposal, not the proposer.
- **Idea Parking Lot:** Write ideas on sticky notes or anonymously in a shared doc during brainstorming. Then evaluate ideas collectively without knowing who offered what. This is useful in early creative phases or in hierarchically sensitive teams.
- **Red Team/Blue Team:** Assign one group to generate ideas and another to test them. Everyone knows their role is temporary and based on function, not ego, which helps normalize critique without personalizing it.
- **Framing the Conversation:** Before offering input, try saying: "Let's assume the idea is brilliant but not fully formed yet. What might help it grow?"

FROM PERFECTION TO GROWTH

Psychological safety flourishes when mistakes and setbacks are treated as learning opportunities rather than failures. A hospital system I worked with transformed their patient safety reporting by shifting from a "Who made the mistake?" approach to a "What can we learn from this?" framework.

Initially, reporting was low because people feared blame. After implementing a non-punitive learning system, reporting increased dramatically, allowing them to address systemic challenges before they caused serious harm.

Growth mindset practices include:

1. Normalizing Mistakes

Leaders who openly discuss their own mistakes and what they learned create permission for others to do the same.

Examples:

- **Leader Storytelling:** In team meetings, leaders regularly share "My Favorite Failure of the Month," a real mistake they made, what they learned, and how they adjusted.
- **Slack Channel or Newsletter Section:** "Lessons Learned" (or a twist: "Lessons Earned") where anyone can share a misstep and insight in a casual, constructive way (e.g., "I launched without QA testing… guess what I'll never skip again?").
- **Mistake Wall (Virtual or Physical):** A board where people anonymously (or publicly) post professional stumbles alongside what they learned, turning errors into badges of growth.
- **First Draft Fridays:** Leaders show an unpolished work-in-progress once a month to reinforce that rough starts are part of the process.

2. After-Action Learning

Offer regular, blame-free reviews focusing on improvement rather than assigning fault.

Examples:

- **Blameless Retros:** After projects (especially the messy ones), hold a review asking:
  - What went well?
  - What didn't go as planned?
  - What do we want to try differently next time? Keep names out of it and focus on systems or conditions that led to results.
- **"Three Truths and a Stretch" Format:** Each team member shares three things that worked well and one area to stretch/improve. This encourages balance and ownership.
- **Rotating Facilitator Role:** Assign a new facilitator for each after-action review to promote shared responsibility for learning, not just leader-led lessons.
- **"What Would You Teach From This?" Prompt:** Have each person suggest what someone else could learn from the project. This shifts the focus from failure to contribution.

3. Celebrating Learning Attempts

Recognizing effort and progress, not just successful outcomes.

Examples:

- **"Best Bold Move" Award:** Monthly team recognition for someone who tried something courageous or new, regardless of the result
- **Progress Celebrations:** Shout-outs in meetings for milestones like:
  - "Launched her first client proposal solo!"
  - "Tried a new format for the report. Even though it didn't land, it sparked a great discussion."
- **Learning Badges:** Create digital or physical "badges" (even silly ones!) to recognize first attempts (e.g., "First Failed Pitch," "Tried It Anyway," or "Idea Adventurer")

- **Retrospective Rituals:** Close projects by highlighting "most improved," "biggest risk taken," or "new skill tested," not just top performance.

4. "Not Yet" Language

Framing challenges as development opportunities rather than fixed limitations.

Examples:

- **Shift from "You can't do this" to:**
    - "You haven't mastered this *yet* — let's look at where you're stuck."
    - "You're still building this skill. Here's what growth looks like."
- **Growth Tracker Boards:** Replace checklists of "done/not done" with progress markers like:
    - "Just starting," "Getting there," "Almost fluent," "Teaching others."
- **Performance Review Prompts:** Include questions like:
    - "What's something you're still learning?"
    - "What would you like to be better at 3 months from now?"
- **Coaching Language:** Use prompts like:
    - "What would moving from 'not yet' to 'getting there' look like?"
    - "What do you think is standing between where you are and where you want to be?"

FROM SPEECH TO COMMUNICATION

True communication is two-way. Many organizations measure engagement by how much they tell employees, failing to create effective channels for hearing from them.

A retail company I worked with prided itself on "transparent communication" because executives regularly shared updates and decisions. But when we surveyed employees, they felt fundamentally unheard because there were no effective channels for their insights to travel upward.

We implemented structured two-way communication through:

Regular listening sessions: Small group discussions where leaders primarily listen rather than speak.

Insight escalation paths: Clear processes for frontline observations to reach decision-makers.

Decision loops: Demonstrating how input influenced decisions, even when the final decision didn't align with all suggestions.

Prioritized response systems: Clear expectations about which communication requires response, from whom, and by when.

Within six months, employee trust scores increased, and the organization implemented several significant operational improvements based on frontline insights that previously had no path to decision-makers.

The ROI: When Belonging Takes Root

The impact of true belonging extends far beyond how people feel. Organizations with strong belonging cultures consistently demonstrate measurable business advantages that affect the bottom line.

Innovation thrives when team members feel psychologically safe to propose unusual ideas and challenge established thinking without fear of ridicule or career penalties. This psychological safety creates an environment where creative solutions emerge from unexpected places, driving competitive advantage. Retention rates dramatically improve as people remain loyal to organizations where they feel genuinely valued for their unique perspectives and contributions rather than merely their compliance with established norms. This reduces costly turnover and preserves institutional knowledge.

Organizations built on belonging also demonstrate remarkable resilience during challenging times because communication flows openly in all directions. Problems surface earlier when people feel safe reporting concerns, and solutions emerge more readily when diverse perspectives are actively sought and incorporated.

Perhaps most significantly, performance metrics consistently improve when people bring their full capabilities to work rather than expending precious mental and emotional energy maintaining carefully managed versions of themselves. As we've seen, this translates to higher productivity, better decision-making, and stronger financial results.

> **TRUTH BOMB**
>
> Creating this culture of belonging requires the consistent practice of transparency, vulnerability, and humanity expressed through everyday communication choices made by leaders at all levels.

In the next two parts, we'll explore how to lead transformational change, building on this foundation of belonging to create sustainable cultural shifts that drive long-term organizational success.

PART 4
DRIVING BREAKTHROUGH TRANSFORMATION

The journey to organizational excellence is about creating the connections and systems that turn vision into reality. In the previous sections, we explored finding your voice and taking the first steps toward creating cultures of belonging. Now we turn to the transformative power of strategic relationship-building and measuring return on investment (ROI) that turns communication into a competitive advantage.

Chapter 7, "The Social Capitalist," reveals how successful leaders leverage their communication currency to build the social capital necessary for meaningful change. Far from being some fluffy, feel-good stuff, relationship-building is the essential infrastructure that determines whether your change initiatives succeed or fail.

By assessing your relationship networks, envisioning concrete change, and applying those three pillars—transparency, vulnerability, and humanity—you can bridge that persistent disconnect between what leaders intend and what employees actually experience. The most powerful transformations happen when leaders differentiate themselves through relationship rather than rhetoric. Build before you need. Invest in connection before requiring support. Because here's what I know after two decades of coaching executives: technical solutions implemented through weak relationships fail, while even imperfect solutions implemented through strong relationships succeed.

In Chapter 8, "Are We Winning or Dominating?" we examine how to measure the success of your communication efforts in ways that directly connect to business outcomes. While most organizations track financial metrics with obsessive precision, those that truly dominate their markets apply that same disciplined measurement to communication effectiveness and cultural alignment.

I'll give you practical frameworks like the Trust Triangle, the Communication Effectiveness Index, and the Communication Balance Sheet so you can demonstrate the return on your investments in culture. Organizations that sustain competitive advantage build communication capabilities that enable adaptability and resilience over time. They don't just check the "culture box" with an annual employee survey that collects digital dust somewhere; they create measurement systems that drive continuous improvement.

Together, these chapters provide your roadmap for transforming your organization through strategic communication that builds genuine connection while delivering measurable results. The difference between merely winning and truly dominating your market lies in your ability to treat relationships as capital and communication as an investment — and to measure both with the rigor they deserve.

Chapter 7
The Social Capitalist

> "People don't care how much you know until they know how much you care."
>
> –Theodore Roosevelt

Okay, reader. It's time to sit up and pay attention. Get out your favorite highlighter or pen and get ready to take some notes because I'm about to drop some serious knowledge in this chapter. Learning how to be a social capitalist is one of the most important skills you can gain to thrive in the workplace today (and it's only getting more important with the introduction of new technology).

Now, you might be looking at me with your head cocked right now, but hear me out. When I talk about being a "social capitalist," I don't mean someone who profits from relationships in a transactional way. I'm talking about leaders who understand that meaningful connection is the most valuable currency in today's business landscape and who invest in it strategically.

The most successful leaders I've worked with have one thing in common: they build impressive relationship networks. They recognize that their ability to influence, transform, and drive change depends less on positional authority and more on the trust and connection they establish with others.

This chapter explores how to leverage authentic communication to build the social capital necessary for meaningful organizational change. We'll examine how to assess your current position, envision the future state you're working toward, implement effective change communication, and bridge the persistent disconnect between leadership intentions and employee experiences.

The Case for Investing in Social Capital

Before diving into how, let's address why social capital matters so dramatically for organizational change.

To understand why social capital matters, let me tell you another story. When I worked for Stonehaven, they were looking to implement a new Enterprise Resource Planning (ERP) system. This huge operational change would result in all of their transportation, planning, and warehousing systems being in one place. Of course, human beings are creatures of habit. Anytime our cheese gets moved, it's a problem. The leadership team knew they had an uphill battle on their hands.

Meanwhile, as the liaison between leadership and technicians, I'd built up a huge store of social capital. I perhaps wasn't the smartest person on the team, and I certainly wasn't the most technical, but I had the ability to connect with people. As a result, the technical people were really receptive to my training and the ERP leadership team took note. They realized I had built a lot of trust and decided to promote me to help others adopt the change.

In today's workforce, change is constant, rapid, and inevitable. This means that social capital is one of the most critical and necessary tools for professionals to develop. As a leader, the ability to influence adaptability while maintaining high morale and high performance is absolutely essential. If you don't connect with people, it's going to be hard or impossible to lead.

What Does Social Capital Look Like?

So, what does social capital look like? It all starts with connection, and when we think about connection, we often associate it with networking. This is where you want to start building that social capital. But there's a reason I say networking is just one letter away from "not working"—when done without intention, it fails to create the connections that truly matter.

Let me share some strategies that transform superficial networking into meaningful social capital:

Focus on Experience, Not Impression

Don't get consumed with what you're going to say or how you'll "wow" someone. Instead, focus on the experience you're providing. When you're authentically present rather than performing, people connect with the real you, and that's far more memorable than any rehearsed elevator pitch.

Be Strategic About Connections

Not every connection deserves equal time and energy. Be intentional about who you're connecting with and why. Ask yourself: "How can I be an asset to this person?" rather than "What can this person do for me?" This shifts your approach from transactional to valuable.

Find Common Ground First

Before diving into business, establish a foundation of connection. What do you share? Perhaps it's an alma mater, an industry challenge, or even a shared appreciation for good coffee. These common denominators create natural bridges between strangers.

Follow Up with Purpose

The 48-hour rule is non-negotiable. Connect within two days (at the very latest) after meeting someone. But don't just send a generic "nice to meet you" message. Your follow-up should remind them why staying connected benefits them. Does this feel transactional? Remind yourself, following up in this way isn't arrogance, it's clarity about your potential value.

Demonstrate Value, Don't Just Claim It

Skip the fan mail approach where you gush about how amazing they are. Instead, show how you might contribute to their success. Share an article relevant to a challenge they mentioned, make a specific introduction, or offer perspective on an issue they're facing.

Build Reciprocity from Day One

The strongest networks evolve through mutual value exchange. Even if you're early in your career, you have something to offer — a fresh perspective, technical skills, or simply genuine enthusiasm. Leading with "How can I help?" establishes the right foundation for lasting connections.

Remember: Social capital is about so much more than collecting business cards and LinkedIn connections. It's about building relationships in which both parties recognize and appreciate the value each brings to the table. When you approach networking as an opportunity to create value rather than extract it, you'll build social capital that pays dividends throughout your career.

Start Where You Are: Assessing Your Social Capital Position

Sure, you can be great at networking beyond your organization, but how's the health of your internal connections? Meaningful change begins with an honest assessment of your current position. When it comes to social capital, you need to evaluate both your personal relationship network and your organization's connection infrastructure.

CONDUCTING A PERSONAL NETWORK ASSESSMENT

Consider your own relationship network within your organization. Map your connections across these dimensions:

Breadth: Do your relationships extend beyond your immediate team or department? Beyond those at your level? Beyond those who share your background?

Depth: With how many people have you established genuine trust versus superficial courtesy?

Reciprocity: Are your relationships primarily transactional ("What can this person do for me?") or genuinely reciprocal?

Access: Can you reach key stakeholders directly, or do you rely on intermediaries?

A client who led engineering at a tech company realized through doing this assessment that while he had deep relationships within his department, he had almost no meaningful connections with marketing, sales, or customer success teams. This explained why his technical innovations often failed to translate into market success — he lacked the social capital to align cross-functional efforts.

ORGANIZATIONAL ASSESSMENT: THE CONNECTION INFRASTRUCTURE

Beyond your personal network, assess your organization's connection infrastructure.

Information Flow Patterns: Does information move freely across departments and levels, or does it remain siloed?

Psychological Safety Indicators: Do people speak candidly about challenges, or is there a culture of artificial harmony?

Decision Visibility: Are decision-making processes transparent or opaque?

Recognition Systems: Do your reward structures incentivize collaboration or internal competition?

Belonging Signals: Do people from diverse backgrounds and with different communication styles feel equally valued?

You can do this as an individual, but it's more powerfully done as a group. One organization I worked with discovered through this assessment that while their executive team had strong connections with each other, middle managers felt disconnected from senior leadership. This created a bottleneck where strategic initiatives stalled during implementation because those responsible for execution lacked context and buy-in.

TURNING ASSESSMENT INTO ACTION

The purpose of these assessments isn't to create elaborate reports (I can hear you yawning already!). It's to identify specific gaps you need to address. When you understand where social capital is lacking, you can invest strategically rather than haphazardly.

Of course, leaders are in the best position to turn assessment into action. For example, if you discover weak connections between departments, you might implement cross-functional projects with shared outcomes. If your assessment reveals low psychological safety, you might focus on creating forums where radical candor receives positive reinforcement.

As an individual contributor, you might be thinking, "this is all well and good, but I'm not in a position to change anything at my organization." It's fair for you to have this reaction; however, what I want you to keep in mind is that social capital building starts with individuals at every level. You don't need a formal leadership title to strengthen connections across your immediate sphere of influence. Begin by mapping your existing relationships, identifying gaps in your network, and taking small, consistent steps to build bridges.

WHAT YOU HAVE CANNOT BE BOUGHT

Some people invest in tangible assets like real estate or vending machines. My capital is social. I'm big on fostering and leveraging meaningful relationships, creating trust, and always asking: "How can everybody win?" This approach has been a game changer for getting to the next level in my career. In fact, it's been my key asset.

This became clear early on when I was working at Ironwood, supporting a senior director in the supply chain for Quaker, Tropicana, and Gatorade. I didn't have the fanciest degree or a long resume at that time — this was probably my second corporate job. But what I did have was the awareness and ability to create meaningful relationships.

The senior executive I was supporting had been impressed by my work. One day he said, "Denise, I love that every time I call your desk, you answer. You're always ready." When he asked me to create a report he needed to present the next morning, I delivered. After he reviewed it, he told me, "I see how you navigate and how you respond. Some of my team members have also said they really appreciate partnering with you. I want you to present because you have influence."

Then he said something that changed my perspective forever: "What you have is not anything that can be bought. You can't buy it. You have to earn it, and you are earning it." This is where I was first introduced to the concept of social capitalism, and it connects to what we discussed about AI earlier. There's no artificial intelligence that can replace relationships.

That conversation with the senior executive not only validated that I needed to continue leaning into communication as a superpower, but it created a relationship where he became my mentor, then my champion in rooms I wasn't even in. Because of that, I was able to enter those rooms myself. People I didn't even know started calling me the "Digital Dashboard Queen."

Throughout my career, every time I got promoted or moved to the next level, I could trace it back to relationships I had nurtured. Whether it's getting a referral to speak on a global stage or being invited to head a major leadership program, that's social capital at work. It's not transactional — it's intentional. It's about making sure the people you collaborate with feel heard, valued, and connected.

Many people don't lean into social capital because they think it's networking and they don't like to network. But social capitalism goes way beyond networking (in a way that I think brings more energy to networking), building a reputation and brand that will always be there, even when you're not in the room. Develop this skill and you'll be regarded as a trusted leader who helps others win and rise.

Even without organizational authority, your personal social capital can create ripple effects that gradually shift team dynamics, improve information flow in your area, and demonstrate the value of strategic relationship-building. Remember, some of the most influential people in organizations aren't those with the fanciest titles; they're those who've built robust networks that allow them to get things done regardless of their position on the org chart.

>  **TRUTH BOMB**
>
> Need some extra inspiration? Post this quote from Heller Keller where you can look at it every day: "The only thing worse than being blind is having sight but no vision."

Envisioning Change: What Do You Want to See Differently?

With a clear understanding of your starting point, the next step is defining where you want to go. Effective change requires not just dissatisfaction with the present, but a compelling vision of the future.

BEYOND GENERIC ASPIRATIONS

Too many change efforts fail because their vision consists of vague aspirations like "better communication" or "increased innovation." These provide insufficient direction for meaningful action.

Instead, define concrete changes in observable behaviors and outcomes:

Instead of: "We want more open communication."

Specify: "We want a culture in which people raise concerns early, ideas are met with curiosity and thoughtful discussion, and information flows across departmental boundaries without requiring formal escalation."

Instead of: "We need to be more innovative."

Specify: "We want to establish practices where cross-functional teams regularly collaborate on customer challenges, failure is treated as a learning opportunity rather than a career risk, and employees at all levels have channels to propose and champion new ideas."

The specificity matters because it creates clear targets for your communication efforts and makes progress measurable.

BALANCING ASPIRATION AND REALITY

While your vision should be ambitious, it must also connect to your organization's reality. This connection between aspiration and practical implementation is critical for credibility and momentum.

I worked with a healthcare leadership team that wanted to accomplish a complete cultural transformation within six months. Their senior leaders were operating at a very macro level — highly goals-oriented and future-focused. While their ambition was commendable, this timeline proved unrealistic and undermined their credibility with frontline staff who lived in the day-to-day operational reality.

We adjusted their approach to focus on celebrating "micro wins" (small, visible changes that could happen relatively quickly and signal meaningful progress). This shift in communication strategy helped sustain momentum and gave people the motivation to stay engaged for the longer-term goals.

>  **TRUTH BOMB**
>
> When communicating change, remember the lens you're looking through. Senior leaders naturally view things from a future-oriented, strategic perspective, while operational staff focus on day-to-day implementation. Effective change communication addresses both viewpoints.

Your vision should stretch but not snap your organization. Consider these three critical factors:

Size and Structure: How large is your organization and how complex are its operational realities? Remember that individual contributors often lack support staff and must implement change while managing their existing workload.

Workforce Transition Reality: Be prepared to accept that 25–30% of your current workforce may exit during significant cultural change. This doesn't signify failure. It's a natural part of meaningful transformation. High performance ultimately comes from cultural alignment and appreciation.

Return on Investment (ROI) Assessment: Is the juice worth the squeeze? In other words, will this cultural change genuinely create higher performance, exceed goals, and increase profitability? Or as I sometimes tell clients, "Focus your energy on things you can actually change and influence, and accept the things you can't."

Most individuals at entry level or individual contributor positions won't feel comfortable speaking up about challenges because they don't want to be seen as troublemakers or disruptors. This makes it absolutely the leader's responsibility to create goals at the macro, visionary level while ensuring the implementation process considers those who feel least empowered to voice concerns.

A vision that acknowledges these realities while still inspiring action will generate far more traction than one that exists in an idealized vacuum.

Change Management Through Authentic Communication

With a clear vision established, how do you move your organization from the current state to your desired future? This is where authentic communication becomes the engine of transformation.

THE UVC METHOD IN ORGANIZATIONAL CHANGE

Remember the Unique Values and Capabilities method we explored in Chapter 3? This approach is a powerful framework for organizational change.

When leading change, start by identifying:

Organizational Values: What core principles guide your organization's choices? What matters deeply to your culture?

Organizational Capabilities: What distinctive strengths does your organization possess? What do you do particularly well?

Change Alignment: How does the desired change connect to and leverage these values and capabilities?

This alignment creates what I call "change resonance": transformation that feels like a natural evolution rather than an artificial imposition.

A manufacturing company I worked with struggled with a quality improvement initiative until they reframed it to connect with their deeply held value of craftsmanship. Rather than focusing on error reduction metrics, they centered their communication on enabling master craftspeople to create their best work. Same objective, but the resonance with existing values created dramatically different engagement.

Think of your company's UVC like this: Suppose you're planning a family vacation to an international location and you booked a cruise to get you to the destination. Unfortunately, two weeks before your trip, the cruise line says there are no ships available and they'll have to refund your money. It's now up to you to find an alternative method of transportation — and quick! What do you do? Well, if you have a strong UVC, you can tap into it and get curious. Ask yourself, how can I still enjoy and appreciate this experience? If you have built strong social capital, you can reach out to your network and connect with a travel agent who can book you a flight at a reasonable rate on short notice or a friend of a friend with a yacht to get you there.

Change management in an organization is just a macro version of change management on an individual level. With a strong UVC, you can navigate change and all the unexpected curves that change tends to throw at us.

THE THREE PILLARS IN ACTION

For leaders, going back to the three pillars can also give you grounding in the midst of messy change. Applying the three pillars, transparency, vulnerability, and humanity, creates the conditions where change can flourish.

1. Transparency: The Foundation for Change

During organizational change, transparency means:

Context Communication: Sharing not just what is changing, but why it's necessary.

Decision Visibility: Making clear how decisions are made and who makes them.

Progress Honesty: Acknowledging both achievements and setbacks rather than spinning narratives.

Timeline Reality: Being forthright about what's known, what's uncertain, and when more information will be available.

A technology company I worked with implemented a major restructuring that initially created significant anxiety. The breakthrough came when the CEO held weekly "state of the transition" sessions where he shared:

- The specific market challenges driving the change
- The decision-making framework being used
- Current status, including both successes and difficulties
- Questions that remained unanswered, with timelines for resolution

While not everyone agreed with every decision, the transparency dramatically reduced resistance because people understood the rationale and felt respected rather than manipulated.

2. Vulnerability: Creating Change Partnership

Leading change is about creating the conditions where collective intelligence can emerge. This requires vulnerability:

Learning Stance: Acknowledging that leaders don't have all the answers and genuinely seeking input.

Mistake Recognition: Openly addressing when change efforts don't proceed as planned.

Personal Impact Sharing: Leaders appropriately discussing how the change affects them personally.

A hospital CEO transformed a stalled electronic health record implementation by sharing her own struggles with the new system. Rather than presenting an image of effortless adaptation, she acknowledged specific challenges she faced, invited others to share their experiences, and positioned the entire organization as learning together. This vulnerability shifted the dynamic from compliance to collaboration.

3. Humanity: Supporting People Through Transition

Change is intellectual in design but emotional in execution. Recognizing the human experience of transition:

Loss Acknowledgment: Recognizing what people may lose in the change, not just what they'll gain.

Emotional Space: Creating forums where people can express concerns without being labeled "resistant."

Individualized Support: Recognizing that people adapt to change at different paces and in different ways.

When a financial services firm consolidated offices, leaders focused exclusively on the benefits of the new location until they realized long-tenured employees were grieving the loss of their workplace community. By creating space to acknowledge this loss, including a formal farewell event for the old office, they helped people process emotions that were blocking their engagement with the new site.

COMMUNICATING THROUGH THE CHANGE CURVE

People navigate change through predictable emotional stages. Your communication approach must adapt to meet people where they are:

Shock/Denial Stage: Focus on clear, consistent repetition of key messages. People absorb limited information during this phase.

Anger/Fear Stage: Emphasize listening and validation over attempting to "correct" emotions. Create safe spaces for expression.

Exploration Stage: Provide specific guidance, resources, and small wins to build momentum and confidence.

Acceptance Stage: Celebrate progress, reinforce changes through stories, and begin building toward the next evolution.

Understanding where different individuals and teams fall on this change curve allows you to customize your communication strategy accordingly. The most effective change leaders don't try to rush people through these stages or ignore emotional responses. Instead, they recognize that each stage requires different types of support and information.

By meeting people where they are—not where you wish they were—you create the psychological safety needed for genuine rather than superficial adoption. Remember that different parts of your organization will move through these stages at different rates, requiring you to maintain multiple communication approaches simultaneously as you guide the entire system toward meaningful transformation.

Bridging the Leadership-Employee Disconnect

Perhaps no challenge undermines change efforts more consistently than the persistent gap between leadership intentions and employee experience. Leaders announce transformative initiatives while employees roll their eyes, having seen similar efforts fade away countless times.

The chasm isn't usually about content — it's about connection.

THE RELATABILITY IMPERATIVE

When I work with senior leaders on change initiatives, many initially believe their expertise alone should drive adoption. "If I explain the business case clearly enough, people will get on board," they tell me.

But in today's workplace, expertise without relatability creates limited influence. People don't follow spreadsheets; they follow leaders they connect with.

Although meaningful relationships are a key component to change management, this does not require any compromise to these relationships or your standards. It means demonstrating that you understand their reality and that your vision connects to their concerns.

Relatable leaders consistently practice:

Reality Recognition: Acknowledging the actual conditions people face rather than an idealized version.

Frontline Exposure: Regularly experiencing the work as it actually happens, not just receiving filtered reports.

Constraint Awareness: Understanding the limitations and challenges that impact implementation.

Value Translation: Connecting organizational priorities to what people value personally.

The power of relatability lies in establishing authentic connection that builds the trust necessary for meaningful change. When leaders take the time to truly understand the day-to-day realities of their teams, they gain insights that reshape their approach to implementation and communication. This investment in relationships makes change more palatable and more effective, as solutions become grounded in practical reality rather than theoretical ideals. In organizations where leaders prioritize relatability alongside expertise, change initiatives move from compliance-based adoption to commitment-driven transformation.

DIFFERENTIATION THROUGH RELATIONSHIP

In a world where most change initiatives sound similar on paper, leaders differentiate themselves through relationships rather than rhetoric.

Consider these contrasting approaches from two otherwise similar financial institutions implementing cybersecurity protocols:

Company A: Issued comprehensive documentation, conducted required training, and monitored compliance metrics.

Company B: Did all of the above, but also had leaders share personal stories about data security incidents that affected them, created cross-functional discussion groups to address implementation challenges, and established regular forums where employees could ask questions without judgment.

Both achieved technical compliance; however, Company B created true cultural change because they invested in relationships alongside requirements.

Leaders who differentiate through relationship consistently:

Build Before Needing: Establish connections during "sunny days" before requiring support for change initiatives.

Create Context Channels: Develop forums specifically designed for two-way communication about strategic context.

Demonstrate Consistency: Align their actions with their messages, particularly when doing so is difficult.

Show Up Human: Bring appropriate personality and vulnerability to their communications rather than hiding behind corporate language.

What separates transformational leaders from merely efficient managers is their ability to create human connection alongside strategic direction. By investing in relationships first — before expecting buy-in — these leaders create the foundation of trust that makes otherwise identical change initiatives succeed where others fail. Organizations where leadership prioritizes relationship-building discover that implementation timelines accelerate, resistance decreases, and innovations emerge from unexpected places. The difference is in how they've established the relational context that allows their message to truly be heard.

Measuring the Return on Social Capital Investment

Like any investment, social capital should generate measurable returns. But many organizations fail to track these outcomes systematically, missing opportunities to demonstrate the business impact of relationships.

Consider tracking these metrics to measure your social capital ROI:

Change Implementation Speed: How quickly do new initiatives move from announcement to full adoption?

Information Travel Time: How long does it take for important information to reach all relevant stakeholders?

Psychological Safety Indicators: Do early warning signals about problems increase over time?

Cross-Functional Collaboration: Do departments work together more effectively on complex challenges?

Recovery Resilience: How quickly does your organization bounce back from setbacks?

Employee Advocacy: Do employees promote your organization to their networks?

A technology company I worked with implemented quarterly "connection scores" that measured relationship strength across departments. They discovered a direct correlation between these scores and project success rates. Teams with stronger cross-functional relationships delivered better outcomes in less time with fewer resources.

Your Social Capital Action Plan

Now it's time to translate these concepts into specific actions. Here's a framework for building your social capital action plan:

1. NETWORK EXPANSION

Identify specific relationship gaps in your organization based on your assessment. Then create deliberate opportunities to build connections.

- Schedule regular cross-functional sessions (e.g., lunches, coffee breaks).
- Informally check in with team members with the question "What do you need from me today in order to thrive?"
- Implement job shadowing or rotation programs.
- Create mixed-team task forces for organizational challenges.
- Establish informal mentoring relationships across departments.

Example: A hospital significantly improved patient care coordination by implementing monthly "understanding your colleague" sessions where different departments explained their workflows to others. These simple exchanges created relationships that facilitated better real-time collaboration.

2. TRUST ACCELERATION

Trust typically builds gradually through repeated interactions, but you can accelerate it through specific practices.

- Create "speed of need" response systems where help requests receive priority.
- Establish clear agreements and visibly keep them.
- Acknowledge mistakes quickly and directly—own your sh*t!
- Demonstrate fairness, especially when it would be easier not to.

Example: One retail organization implemented a "no meeting is optional" policy — if someone was invited, it meant their input was genuinely needed. This simple practice dramatically increased trust by eliminating the common experience of being included as a formality.

3. COMMUNICATION ENHANCEMENT

Identify and address communication gaps that prevent relationship development.

- Create information-sharing rituals that cross organizational boundaries.
- Build communication channels that invite honest contributions and that people will actually use.
- Develop common language around key priorities and values.
- Implement communication technology that connects rather than isolates.

Example: A manufacturing company transformed their culture by replacing their traditional suggestion box (which rarely received submissions) with "improvement huddles" (brief, regular conversations where teams identified small changes that would make work better). These face-to-face interactions built relationships while improving operations.

4. RECOGNITION ALIGNMENT

Ensure your recognition systems reinforce rather than undermine relationship building.

- Celebrate collaborative achievements, not just individual heroics.
- Recognize relationship-building behaviors, not just task completion.
- Share stories and experiences that highlight successful cross-functional partnerships.
- Create incentives for knowledge sharing and supporting others' success.

Example: A financial services firm adjusted their annual awards program to require that nominations include examples of how the person supported others' success. This simple criterion shifted behavior throughout the year as people recognized that helping others succeed advanced their own recognition opportunities.

The Social Capitalist's Truth

Throughout my years working with organizations navigating significant change, I've observed this consistent truth: technical solutions implemented through weak relationships fail, while even imperfect solutions implemented through strong relationships succeed.

The most successful leaders understand that social capital is a "must have" that makes work more pleasant. It's the essential infrastructure that enables everything else to function. Just as financial capital makes business operations possible, social capital makes business transformation achievable.

As you consider your own change initiatives, remember that the time you invest in building genuine connections isn't a distraction from the "real work." It is the real work. The strength of your relationships will determine the success of your strategies more predictably than any other factor.

In the next chapter, we'll explore how to measure success in organizational culture transformation, focusing on metrics that matter beyond traditional Key Performance Indicators (KPIs).

Chapter 8
Are we Winning or Dominating?

> "Above all, success in business requires two things: a winning competitive strategy, and superb organizational execution. Distrust is the enemy of both. I submit that while high trust won't necessarily rescue a poor strategy, low trust will almost always derail a good one."
>
> –Stephen M.R. Covey, author of The Speed of Trust: The One Thing That Changes Everything

As my dear friend, gracious writer of the foreword for this book, and author of The Speed of Trust, reminds us, success requires having better ideas than our competitors and executing on those ideas at the highest level.

Success in business doesn't always look the way we think it should. Over the years, I've worked with plenty of organizations that hit their financial targets yet remained plagued by turnover, disengagement, and cultural dysfunction. Conversely, I've seen companies weather significant business challenges while maintaining remarkable team cohesion and resilience because they measured and valued the right things.

The distinction comes down to this: are you merely winning, or are you dominating your space? Winning means hitting your numbers this quarter. Dominating means building an organization that consistently outperforms competitors across multiple dimensions — financial performance, absolutely, but also, talent acquisition and retention, innovation, and adaptability.

The key difference? Organizations that dominate understand that culture is a measurable business asset that drives sustainable results.

They recognize that effective communication directly impacts every aspect of performance, and they measure it with the same rigor they apply to financial metrics.

This chapter explores how to measure the success of your communication and cultural initiatives in ways that connect directly to business outcomes. We'll examine specific metrics that matter, methods for tracking them, and approaches to demonstrating the return on your investments (ROI) in communication and culture.

Stop Guessing, Start Measuring

I sometimes hear from executives:

"Culture is difficult to measure."

Or "Denise, I see how effective communication can help us convey our vision, but how do we measure the impact on our culture?"

The reality is we absolutely can measure culture, and it requires looking at the right indicators. Just as comprehensive financial analysis examines revenue alongside expenses, cash flow, and profitability, cultural measurement requires looking at the indicators that reveal how well people can perform at their best, consistently, over time.

Effective measurement starts with recognizing what you're really trying to accomplish. Cultural transformation is about creating conditions in which people can perform at their best, consistently, over time. The metrics that matter are those that connect to this fundamental purpose. Happiness will follow organically — that's the bonus!

THE ALIGNMENT ADVANTAGE

Organizations with high cultural alignment, where values are clear and consistently lived, outperform their competitors by significant margins. A Gallup survey found that employees who strongly agree with the statement, "I feel connected to my organization's culture" are:

- 4.3 times as likely to be engaged at work.
- 5.3 times as likely to recommend their company as a great place to work.
- 62% less likely to feel burned out at work.
- 47% less likely to be watching for job opportunities or actively looking for another job than their colleagues.[40]

And we know that teams with strong cultural alignment deliver projects faster using fewer resources than teams with low alignment scores, even when controlling for technical skill and experience. According to a McKinsey report, culturally aligned teams used 15–20% fewer resources (time, budget, and personnel) to achieve project goals compared to misaligned teams.[41]

Teams with high alignment also spend less time navigating internal friction, recover more quickly from setbacks, and retain institutional knowledge more effectively because of lower turnover. The cumulative effect creates a substantial competitive advantage.

However, you can only discover connections like this if your organization is first actively measuring both cultural indicators and performance outcomes, then analyzing the relationship between them. Let's jump into how we can make those critical connections.

---

[40] "Organizational Culture," *Gallup*, 2025 (https://www.gallup.com/471521/indicator-organizational-culture.aspx).

[41] "The State of Organizations 2023," *McKinsey & Company*, (https://www.mckinsey.com/~/media/mckinsey/business%20functions/people%20and%20organizational%20performance/our%20insights/the%20state%20of%20organizations%202023/the-state-of-organizations-2023.pdf).

Creating Sustainable Cultural Shifts: Metrics That Matter

Sustainable cultural change requires more than temporary enthusiasm generated by a leadership offsite or new initiative announcement. It needs systematic measurement across multiple dimensions to identify both progress and potential regression points.

THE FOUR BEAT DROPS OF CULTURAL MEASUREMENT

Effective cultural measurement tracks indicators across four key dimensions:

1. The Communication Vibe Check

More than just messages sent, this measures if your words actually land. Are people vibing with your vision or tuning out? This tracks alignment across levels, how fast information flows, and whether decision loops are fire or fizzling.

Consider adding the following areas to your dashboard:

- Message alignment across organizational levels
- Information flow speed and accuracy
- Quality and rhythm of check-ins
- Cross-functional communication effectiveness

2. The Behavior Bassline

Actions speak louder than company values posters. This measures if people are walking the talk, how decisions get made when no one's watching, how conflicts get handled, and whether innovation is flowing or frozen.

Track the following areas:

- Values-aligned decision-making
- Conflict resolution approaches
- Innovation and risk behavior
- Accountability practices

3. The Operational Remix (my personal favorite)

This is where culture meets execution. We track how your people-powered systems actually perform — are cross-functional teams collaborating or clashing? Does change implementation soar or stall? Is resource allocation strategic or scattered?

Keep a close eye on:

- Process adherence and outcomes.
- Cross-functional collaboration.
- Change implementation effectiveness.
- Resource allocation efficiency.

4. The Business Beat Drop

Finally, you get the ultimate payoff track — where culture shows up in results that matter. This measures talent retention, customer loyalty, innovation output, and financial performance. When these metrics are bumping, you know your culture is making money moves.

Add the following metrics to your dashboard:

- Talent acquisition and retention
- Customer experience and loyalty
- Innovation output
- Financial performance

When you measure across all four dimensions, you're tracking the full spectrum of how culture transforms from conversation to cash flow. This is how you know if you're truly dominating your market.

A systematic approach to measurement can yield impressive results. For example, a retail organization implementing a quarterly cultural dashboard across these dimensions could expect to demonstrate, within 18 months, correlations between improved communication effectiveness and measurable business outcomes like reduced inventory costs, faster new product launches, and increased customer satisfaction scores.

The key to success is measurement discipline: consistently tracking the same metrics over time, scrutinizing the relationships between them, and making targeted interventions based on the data.

LEADING VERSUS LAGGING INDICATORS

When tracking finances, there are leading indicators like the number of leads acquired, customer acquisition costs, and cash flow projections and lagging indicators like revenue, net profit or loss, and customer lifetime value. Strong measurement frameworks distinguish between leading and lagging indicators, whether you're tracking finances or culture:

Leading indicators signal future outcomes. For measuring culture, these include:

- Manager communication effectiveness scores.
- Meeting effectiveness ratings.
- Psychological safety measures.
- Information flow metrics.
- Decision transparency ratings.

Lagging indicators confirm what has already happened. For measuring culture, these include:

- Employee turnover.
- Customer satisfaction scores.
- Market share changes.
- Financial performance.

The most effective measurement approaches focus on leading indicators that predict lagging outcomes. This allows for intervention before problems manifest in business results.

When organizations apply this approach systematically, they often discover powerful correlations. A financial services company, for instance, might find that their "decision clarity" metric (measuring how clearly employees understand decision rationales) strongly predicts subsequent implementation speed. By focusing on improving this single leading indicator, they could expect to reduce implementation timelines across major initiatives.

The Measurement Cadence

Cultural measurement must balance comprehensiveness with practicality. I recommend this approach for people leaders:

Daily: Daily check-ins (especially for your younger generations).

Weekly: Quick-pulse checks on team communication effectiveness and psychological safety.

Monthly: Department-level assessments of information flow, collaboration effectiveness, and value alignment.

Quarterly: Organization-wide measurement of cultural indicators, with analysis of connections to operational and business outcomes.

Annually: Comprehensive culture assessment with targeted improvement plans based on identified gaps.

Note that effective measurement goes beyond surveys alone. Organizations should employ multiple methods to gather comprehensive insights:

- Focus groups that provide deeper context.
- One-on-one interviews that reveal individual perspectives.
- Observation of meeting dynamics and informal interactions.
- Analysis of communication patterns through existing data.
- Pulse checks through brief, targeted questions integrated into regular workflows.

This cadence combined with a variety of measurement methods creates continuous visibility into cultural trends while avoiding survey fatigue. Plus, when you combine quantitative survey data with qualitative insights from conversations and behavioral observations, you create a more complete picture of your cultural reality. This multi-method approach allows organizations to identify challenges early while still providing regular deeper analysis of systemic patterns.

Building Trust Across Organizational Levels: Trust as a Metric

Trust is a directly measurable asset that impacts everything from information flow to innovation to execution speed. Organizations with high trust environments outperform low-trust competitors by as much as 286% in total return to shareholders.[42]

THE TRUST TRIANGLE METRIC

I use a "Trust Triangle" measurement approach with clients, to evaluate three types of beliefs essential to organizational trust:

1. **Competence Trust:** Belief that others have the capability to deliver what they promise.
2. **Integrity Trust**: Belief that others will do what they say and act according to stated values.
3. **Care Trust:** Belief that others have your interests in mind, not just their own.

When measured across organizational levels, these dimensions reveal critical gaps that impact performance. For example, when employees give high scores on leadership competence, but lower scores on integrity and care, you may see strategic initiatives failing to gain traction. This could indicate that while employees believe leaders can execute changes, they doubt their motivations and commitments to stated values.

The solution? Design programs that result in and encourage leaders to practice increased transparency and more consistent communication. Then measure and compare integrity and care scores again to ensure that trust improves in those areas.

---

[42] Randy Illig, "A High-Trust Sales Organization Starts from the Top," *Forbes*, October 23, 2018 (https://www.forbes.com/sites/randyillig/2018/10/23/a-high-trust-sales-organization-starts-from-the-top).

CROSS-LEVEL TRUST MEASUREMENT

Trust must flow in multiple directions—not just top-down, but also bottom-up and across functions. Comprehensive trust measurement captures these dimensions:

Upward Trust: How much employees trust their leaders.

Downward Trust: How much leaders trust their teams to deliver.

Lateral Trust: How much departments trust each other to support mutual success.

A manufacturing company I advised discovered they had strong downward trust but weak lateral trust between operations and sales. This trust gap created significant inefficiencies as each department built elaborate verification processes rather than relying on each other's information. By implementing cross-functional trust-building initiatives with specific measurement targets, they reduced order processing time and dramatically improved customer delivery experience.

Measuring Communication Impact on Talent: The Talent Lifecycle

Communication effectiveness directly impacts every stage of the talent lifecycle, from attracting candidates to retaining and developing top performers. Organizations that excel in this area track specific metrics at each stage.

RECRUITMENT RADAR: ARE YOUR HIRING SIGNALS GETTING THROUGH?

1. Heard Loud and Clear?" – The Candidate Vibe Check

Think of this as your recruitment Yelp rating. How do candidates feel about the journey—the clarity, the pace, the human-ness of it all? Are they ghosted, looped in, or left wondering if the interview was real or a dream?

Metrics to watch: Candidate input surveys given post-interview or post-application.

2. Message in a Bottle, or Billboard? – Brand Signal Strength

Does your brand whisper one thing on LinkedIn, shout another on Glassdoor, and post memes on Instagram that don't match either? This checks how consistently you're telling the same story across platforms.

Inconsistent messaging creates confusion and mistrust among potential candidates. When your LinkedIn posts about 'work-life balance' contradict employee reviews on Glassdoor describing burnout culture, top talent notices. Candidates research companies across multiple touchpoints before applying, and mixed messages signal either a lack of self-awareness or, worse, intentional misrepresentation. Consistent brand messaging builds credibility and attracts candidates who align with your actual culture rather than those drawn to false promises.

Metrics to watch: Content audits and candidate perception surveys.

3. "They Said Yes!" – The Offer Acceptance Spark

A strong yes rate says you've nailed the courtship — clarity, enthusiasm, and mutual understanding. A meh or missing yes means something got lost in translation.

Metrics to watch: Percentage of extended offers that get signed.

4. Culture Chemistry – The Afterparty Test

This is the "How's it going *after* the honeymoon?" metric. Are your new hires thriving in the environment you promised? Or are they wondering if they joined the wrong band?

Metrics to watch: Retention at 90/180 days, engagement scores, culture-fit pulse checks.

A professional services firm I worked with discovered their offer acceptance rate was below industry average despite competitive compensation. Through targeted interviews, they learned candidates were receiving inconsistent messages about the firm's culture and expectations during the interview process. After implementing a structured communication approach for interviewers, their acceptance rate increased within two quarters.

> **TIME OUT**
>
> I know this is a lot of metrics to track at once! Don't feel like you need to implement all of these tomorrow. The reality is that most organizations are already drowning in data — what you need is focus.
>
> Pick 2–3 metrics that feel most relevant to your current talent challenges and start there. Are you struggling to get good candidates to say yes to offers? Focus on the recruitment metrics. Is turnover your biggest headache? Zero in on the retention indicators. The goal is progress, not perfection, and measuring consistently in a few areas beats sporadically tracking everything.

ARE WE KEEPING THE BAND TOGETHER? TALENT RETENTION METRICS THAT ACTUALLY TELL A STORY

1. Mic'd Up or Muffled? – Manager Message Check

Are managers crystal-clear or cryptic? This looks at how well they set expectations, offer guidance, and throw some well-deserved high-fives.

Metrics to watch: *Employee pulse surveys on manager clarity, one-to-one effectiveness, and recognition frequency.*

2. "Where Are We Even Going?" – Strategic Clarity Test

Do your people feel like co-pilots or passengers on this company rocket ship? This shows whether employees understand not just *what* they do, but *why* it matters.

Metrics to watch: *Survey results on mission clarity and role alignment with goals.*

3. "Is This Thing On?" – The Voice Check

Are suggestions falling into the void, or actually sparking change? This one checks whether people believe their voices matter — or if your so-called "listening channels" are just decorative.

Metrics to watch: *Perceived influence scores, common themes from employee input, participation in town halls or innovation initiatives.*

4. Standing Ovation or Slow Clap? – Recognition That Lands

Recognition shouldn't feel like an automated birthday email from a bot. This asks you to consider whether praise is timely and genuine, and whether it hits home.

Metrics to watch: *Recognition sentiment, frequency, and impact on engagement scores.*

A technology company implemented quarterly measurement of these metrics and discovered their "voice perception" scores were consistently low across departments. Employees didn't believe their input mattered. By creating structured listening channels and demonstrating how employee input influenced decisions, they reduced voluntary turnover over 18 months.

IS THE FIRE STILL LIT? TALENT ENGAGEMENT METRICS THAT GO BEYOND FREE SNACKS AND PING-PONG

1. Speak Freely or Smile and Nod? – The Psychological Safety Scan

Is your team brave enough to say, "Hey, this might flop"? Or are people quietly disengaging behind polite head nods? This is one of the indicators of an effective culture that often feels hard to measure, but psychological safety is not just a vibe.

Metrics to watch: *Survey results on comfort sharing dissenting views, raising risks, or admitting mistakes without fear.*

2. Info or Inbox Overload? – The Clarity Radar

Are people informed or just overwhelmed? This tracks whether employees get the *right* info at the *right* time to do great work — not just another All-Staff update that nobody reads.

Metrics to watch: Survey data on communication clarity, usefulness of internal resources, and perceived support.

3. Purpose Pulse – Do They Know Why It Matters?

Do your people see the impact of their work, or are they just ticking boxes? This is the heartbeat of engagement — knowing you're building *something bigger*.

Metrics to watch: Connection-to-purpose scores, storytelling touchpoints, and qualitative insights from one-on-ones or stay interviews.

4. Cross-Team Mojo – Collaboration Without the Chaos

Is collaboration seamless or like herding caffeinated cats? This measures whether teams actually *work together* — or just bump into each other in Slack.

Metrics to watch: Insights on ease of collaboration, tool effectiveness, and team-to-team trust.

5. Legacy Mode Unlocked – The Succession Signal

Are your high performers just sprinting solo, or thinking like legacy-builders? This tracks whether people are cultivating others, codifying wisdom, and creating something that lasts beyond them.

Metrics to watch: Internal talent pipeline strength, knowledge transfer practices, mentorship engagement, and readiness ratings.

A retail organization discovered that while their "purpose connection" scores were high, "information adequacy" scores were consistently low. Employees understood and believed in the company mission but lacked the specific information needed to make good decisions. By implementing targeted information-sharing practices, they improved customer service scores within six months.

THE BOTTOM LINE: YOUR TALENT COMMUNICATION SCORECARD

If you're struggling with...	Focus on these metrics first:
Low offer acceptance rates	Candidate experience surveys, brand message consistency
High early turnover (0–6 months)	Manager communication effectiveness, culture fit pulse checks
Disengaged long-term employees	Voice perception scores, purpose connection, psychological safety
Poor cross-team collaboration	Information adequacy, team-to-team trust, collaboration effectiveness
Weak leadership pipeline	Knowledge transfer practices, mentorship engagement, succession readiness

Remember: Start small, measure consistently, and use the data to drive targeted improvements. The most successful organizations don't track everything—they track what matters most for solving their specific talent challenges.

Measuring the Return on Investment (ROI) of Communication Initiatives

This section is dedicated to all the finance gurus, the spreadsheet sorcerers, the Excel whisperers. For all my finance people, I see you and I didn't forget about you.

When executives ask me to help them see why they should invest in communication initiatives, they're essentially asking about

ROI—return on investment. The challenge is connecting "soft" communication improvements to "hard" business outcomes. This connection becomes clear when you measure the right things in the right ways.

Effective communication, leadership development, and coaching aren't just feel-good programs—they directly address the root causes of disengagement, low morale, and leadership breakdowns. When leaders can't deliver direction clearly or navigate tough conversations, the ripple effects hit productivity, trust, and retention. Strategic communication helps bridge these gaps, preventing workplace fires before they spread.

From a measurable ROI standpoint, I communicate to my clients that:

- You will see an increase in team performance.
- You will see a decrease in constant revisions and constant repeating because you now have clear communication.

From a cost-savings perspective, I tell them that:

- You're going to see a reduction in turnover—multiply that from a quantitative standpoint.
- You'll also see an improvement in productivity.

There's another factor many organizations overlook: internal promotion rates. Companies are shifting away from a heavy focus on talent acquisition and toward paying more attention to talent retention.

The return on investment (ROI) of communication coaching has everything to do with using communication to drive performance and build trust so that people don't want to leave. When you develop your existing talent through better communication, you reduce recruiting costs while building institutional knowledge and stronger team cohesion.

In short, strong communication is a business multiplier that touches every aspect of organizational performance.

THE COMMUNICATION-REVENUE CONNECTION

Organizations with effective communication practices outperform those with poor communication by substantial margins. One study found that companies with highly effective communicators had 47% higher total returns to shareholders over five years compared to companies with less effective communicators.[43]

To demonstrate this connection in your organization, track these relationships:

1. Communication Clarity → Process Efficiency

Measure the relationship between how clearly initiatives are communicated and subsequent implementation costs. A manufacturing client found that projects with high communication clarity scores required fewer resources to implement than those with low clarity scores.

2. Input Quality → Innovation Rate

Track how the quality and frequency of guidance and idea exchange correlate with innovation outcomes. A technology company discovered that teams receiving structured, timely input produced more viable product innovations than teams with irregular communication and review processes.

3. Leadership Communication → Employee Retention

Measure the impact of leadership communication effectiveness on retention of high performers. A healthcare organization found that departments with highly rated leadership communication retained more top talent annually than departments with poor leadership communication.

4. Cross-Functional Communication → Time to Market

Assess how effectively departments communicate with each other and its impact on product development timelines. A consumer goods

---

43 Robert Sher, "Never Leave Internal Communications to Chance in Midsized Companies," *Forbes*, July 17, 2014 (https://www.forbes.com/sites/robertsher/2014/07/17/never-leave-internal-communications-to-chance-in-midsized-companies).

company reduced time to market by improving cross-functional communication processes.

COST-OF-POOR-COMMUNICATION ANALYSIS

Another effective approach to clarifying the return on investment (ROI) is by calculating the cost of poor communication. There are several expenses directly attributable to communication failures:

Category	Description	Example Cost Drivers
Rework Costs	Work done improperly the first time due to unclear guidance or information	Labor redundancy, missed deadlines, product recalls
Decision Delay Costs	Time lost due to lack of clear data, missed context, or waiting on responses	Missed market opportunities, delayed product launches
Conflict Resolution	Time/money spent managing avoidable disputes or misunderstandings	Mediation sessions, manager time, legal costs
Knowledge Transfer Failures	Knowledge lost when not documented/ shared correctly	Time spent recreating documents, rehiring/training for knowledge gaps

A *Harvard Business Review* article reveals that poor internal communication costs U.S. organizations $2 trillion annually in lost productivity — a figure that dwarfs most other business inefficiencies. Unlike hypothetical examples, this research provides concrete evidence that communication investments deliver measurable returns far exceeding traditional 7:1 ROI assumptions.[44]

---

[44] "Why Overhauling Internal Communications Could Be Your Greatest Revenue Driver," *Harvard Business Review*, May 11, 2023 (https://hbr.org/sponsored/2023/05/why-overhauling-internal-communications-could-be-your-greatest-revenue-driver).

The data demonstrates that organizations treating internal communication as a strategic business investment rather than an operational expense achieve 23% higher profits and 55% revenue growth compared to less collaborative counterparts. This represents a fundamental shift from viewing communication as a cost center to recognizing it as a primary revenue driver.[45]

THE COMMUNICATION BALANCE SHEET

To make communication make *cents*, let's look at it like any good financial statement—with both assets and liabilities. Great communication builds equity. Poor communication? That's an expense line with compound interest.

Communication Assets	Communication Liabilities
Time Savings Faster alignment reduces meeting time, rework, and clarification loops	**Expectation Misalignment** Leads to rework, scope creep, and frustration
Customer Relationship Growth Clear messaging builds trust, loyalty, and lifetime value	**Slower Decision-Making** Confusion delays action, especially at critical moments
Implementation Acceleration Teams move faster with fewer roadblocks or misinterpretations	**Trust Degradation** Inconsistency or silence erodes confidence in leadership
Talent Retention Employees who feel heard and informed are more likely to stay	**Employee Disengagement** Lack of clarity makes work feel meaningless or chaotic

---

45 "Why Overhauling Internal Communications Could Be Your Greatest Revenue Driver," *Harvard Business Review*, May 11, 2023 (https://hbr.org/sponsored/2023/05/why-overhauling-internal-communications-could-be-your-greatest-revenue-driver).

Communication Assets	Communication Liabilities
Conflict Cost Reduction Proactive communication prevents costly internal disputes	**Knowledge Hoarding** Silos and unclear channels block essential information flow
Discretionary Effort Boost People go above and beyond when they understand the "why"	**Change Resistance** Poor communication fuels fear, rumor mills, and pushback

Companies using this approach have discovered that their communication liabilities were growing faster than their assets, creating significant drag on performance. This aligns with industry reports. One study found that the annual productivity loss per worker due to ineffective communication is $15,000. That's the equivalent of 7.47 hours in lost productivity weekly.[46]

The $15,000 per employee problem emerges as the article's most striking finding. This represents the annual productivity loss per worker due to ineffective communication, equivalent to 7.47 hours of lost productivity weekly. For a 100-employee organization, this translates to $1.5 million in annual losses — before considering turnover costs that can reach $2.6 million annually for the same company size.[47]

THE COMMUNICATION P&L STATEMENT

If the balance sheet is your long-term view, the P&L tracks the *day-to-day health* of your communication. Where are you generating value? Where are you bleeding resources? And is your team operating in the black or in the red?

---

[46] Anna Stallman and Jeremiah Shirk, "How to Foster a Culture of Authentic Internal Communicators," *PRNews*, October 20, 2023 (https://www.prnewsonline.com/how-to-foster-a-culture-of-authentic-internal-communicators).

[47] "Why Overhauling Internal Communications Could Be Your Greatest Revenue Driver," *Harvard Business Review*, May 11, 2023 (https://hbr.org/sponsored/2023/05/why-overhauling-internal-communications-could-be-your-greatest-revenue-driver).

Communication Revenue (The Upside)	Communication Costs (The Downside)
Fewer Meetings Because people understood the first time	Rework Due to misunderstood instructions
On-Time, On-Scope Delivery Projects stay on track when everyone's on the same page	Conflict Escalation Requires manager or HR intervention when issues fester
Referral-Ready Clients People refer you when they feel heard and respected	Burnout Triggered by unclear priorities and mixed signals
Trusted Leadership Leaders who communicate clearly inspire alignment and follow-through	Delayed Decisions Caused by vague ownership or responsibility gaps
Self-Managing Teams Empowered teams course-correct without handholding	Lost Opportunities Because someone didn't speak up — or wasn't heard

In short: if communication were currency, would your culture be cash-flow positive?

Practical Measurement Approaches: Getting Started

Implementing comprehensive measurement may seem daunting, but you can start with focused approaches that deliver immediate value while building toward more sophisticated systems.

Communication Effectiveness Index Worksheet

Measure the impact of your internal communication — quickly and clearly.

How to Use

Rate each of the five elements of communication on a 1 to 5 scale, where: **1 = Poor   3 = Adequate   5 = Excellent**

Gather scores through team pulse surveys, one-on-one check-ins, or manager reflections. Track your composite score over time and look for patterns in relation to team performance, project delays, or employee engagement.

COMMUNICATION ELEMENTS

Element	Guiding Question	Rating (1–5)
Clarity	Do people understand what's being communicated?	
Consistency	Is messaging consistent across channels and leaders?	
Context	Is enough background provided to support understanding and alignment?	
Timeliness	Is information shared when it's needed — not too early, not too late?	
Actionability	Do communications lead to clear, doable next steps?	

Composite Score

Add your ratings from above (maximum score = 25):
Total Score: ___ / 25

INTERPRETATION:

- **0–12** → **Needs Work**
- **13–18** → **Functional**
- **19–22** → **Effective**
- **23–25** → **Excellent**

Tip: Repeat this survey quarterly or after major communications to evaluate effectiveness over time.

When organizations implement this measurement approach, they create a decision loop that drives continuous improvement. The index provides both a baseline for comparison and specific areas to target for intervention. As teams see improvements in their communication metrics, they become more invested in the measurement process itself, creating positive momentum. The real power of this approach lies in its simplicity and focus — by measuring just these five dimensions consistently, organizations can identify precise communication gaps and address them before they impact broader business performance.

THE MEETING EFFECTIVENESS METRIC

Given that meetings consume substantial organizational resources, measuring their effectiveness provides immediate insight into communication health:

Preparation Quality: Were materials provided in advance? Was the purpose clear?

Participation Balance: Did all voices have an opportunity to contribute?

Decision Clarity: Were decisions clearly made and documented?

Action Assignment: Were next steps clearly assigned with ownership and deadlines?

Time Respect: Did the meeting start and end on time? Was the time well used?

When organizations track these metrics consistently, they quickly identify specific areas for improvement in their meeting culture. Decision clarity often emerges as a particular challenge area, with team members leaving discussions without a shared understanding of what was decided. Simple documentation practices like end-of-meeting summaries or digital decision logs can transform meeting effectiveness. The resulting improvements in implementation speed and reduction in follow-up meetings demonstrate how small changes in communication practices can yield significant operational benefits.

THE COMMUNICATION NETWORK ANALYSIS

This approach maps information flow across your organization, identifying bottlenecks and isolated groups:

1. Survey employees about who they regularly communicate with for different types of information.
2. Map these connections visually to identify patterns.
3. Identify critical connectors, bottlenecks, and isolated groups.
4. Target interventions to improve network effectiveness.

A technology company discovered through this analysis that critical product information was flowing through just two key individuals, creating substantial vulnerability. By implementing structural changes to broaden these information pathways, they reduced development delays substantially.

The Metrics That Matter Most

While your specific measurement approach should adapt to your organizational context, certain metrics consistently demonstrate strong predictive power for overall performance:

1. Decision Transparency

Measure how clearly employees understand how and why decisions are made. This single metric strongly predicts implementation effectiveness and employee engagement.

2. Psychological Safety

Track whether people feel safe speaking up about concerns, ideas, and mistakes. This metric predicts innovation capacity and problem prevention effectiveness.

3. Information Flow Speed

Measure how quickly critical information moves to those who need it. This metric predicts responsiveness to market changes and operational efficiency.

4. Manager Communication Effectiveness

Assess how well managers translate organizational direction into team-level clarity. This metric strongly predicts employee performance and retention.

5. Cross-Functional Collaboration Quality

Measure how effectively departments work together on complex challenges. This metric predicts innovation outcomes and operational excellence.

A healthcare system I advised focused intensively on improving their psychological safety metrics, moving from bottom-quartile to top-quartile performance within 18 months. This improvement correlated with an increase in reported near-misses (preventing potential errors) and an increase in process improvement suggestions being implemented.

> **TIME OUT**
>
> Let's pause and make sure we don't lose sight of the human element in all of this.
>
> What I'm observing, both through client work and when people approach me after keynote speaking engagements, is a troubling pattern. People are getting emotional when they share what's really happening in their workplaces. Employers are experiencing quiet quitters, increased turnover, and low morale. For the most part, people are tired of meetings because they can't get work done, and they're burned out from navigating competing priorities.
>
> But here's what's most concerning: people are afraid of speaking up. There are a lot of people right now navigating fear of being fired or being blamed when they're on a highly visible project. This fear has created a mindset where people don't want to take risks anymore. We all know that taking risks is what ultimately leads to innovation, but people aren't in that mindset anymore.

> I've had clients tell me, "When I say things like 'get it done,' I'm realizing that it's shutting people down. I thought I was being efficient and giving people autonomy, but I'm not seeing engagement." It's about intention versus impact. It's rather tone-deaf when you're telling people to "get it done" because in all aspects of life, people are feeling like they're being shouted at and dictated to.
>
> Psychological safety has been at the forefront of my work, and my communication strategies now focus on how to create and sustain it in the workplace. It really has everything to do with demonstrating compassion through active listening, leading with curiosity versus making assumptions, and leading without controlling. These are the practices that can truly create and sustain psychological safety in today's challenging work environment.

Getting Beyond the Measurement Trap

While measurement is essential, I've also seen organizations fall into what I call the "measurement trap" — collecting data without taking meaningful action. Effective measurement systems follow these principles:

1. Measure to Improve, Not to Prove

Focus measurements on identifying improvement opportunities rather than justifying past decisions.

2. Connect Metrics to Actions

Every metric should have clear ownership and a defined response process when it indicates problems.

3. Open Up the Data

Share measurement results broadly to create organizational awareness and ownership of improvement.

4. Celebrate Progress, Not Just Achievement

Recognize meaningful improvement, not just the achievement of targets.

5. Evolve Your Measurement Approach

Regularly review whether you're measuring what truly matters as your organization evolves.

When organizations implement these principles, measurement becomes a catalyst for continuous improvement rather than just a reporting exercise. Teams begin to see metrics as tools for growth rather than instruments of evaluation. This shift in perspective transforms how people engage with the measurement process — from passive subjects to active participants in organizational development. The most powerful measurement approaches create ownership at all levels, with everyone understanding how their contributions impact key metrics and feeling empowered to drive positive change.

The Ultimate Measure: Sustained Competitive Advantage

Your communication and culture effectiveness demonstrates its greatest value through sustained competitive advantage — the capacity to dominate your market over time through capabilities others can't easily replicate. Organizations with strong communication fundamentals demonstrate remarkable resilience during disruption and adaptability during market shifts.

I once worked with two similar-sized companies in the same industry facing the identical market disruption. The company with higher communication effectiveness (i.e., increased transparency, vulnerability, and frequency) scores navigated the change with minimal customer and talent loss, while their competitor experienced significant turnover and customer attrition. Three years later, the first company had grown their market share, while the second was still struggling to regain their previous position.

Although both had strategic attempts resulting in comparable strategic responses, the difference was execution enabled by communication effectiveness — the ability to align people quickly, maintain cohesion during uncertainty, and adapt rapidly as conditions evolved.

This is the ultimate return on investment (ROI) of communication excellence — not just winning today, but dominating your market over time through organizational capabilities your competitors can't easily replicate.

In the final part of this book, we'll explore how to future-proof your communication approach, preparing for continued disruption while maintaining the human connection that technology alone cannot provide.

PART 5
THE FUTURE OF ORGANIZATIONAL COMMUNICATION

In my 20+ years coaching leaders, I've witnessed a pattern: the companies and individuals who dominate their fields aren't just those with momentary success. They're the ones who create sustainable communication practices that allow them to adapt, evolve, and emerge stronger through disruption.

As I tell my clients: winning today is good, but building the capacity to win consistently over time is what separates the truly exceptional from the merely competent.

This final part isn't about quick fixes or temporary solutions. It's about building communication sustainability and resilience that serves you through changing markets, evolving workplace norms, technological disruption, and whatever other challenges emerge along your leadership journey.

Chapter 9, "Sustainability and Resilience," explores how to create communication practices that remain effective even when circumstances change dramatically. You'll learn how to build sustainable leadership communication that conserves your energy while maximizing your impact, how to create organizational communication systems that anticipate needs rather than just responding to problems, and how to leverage technology while maintaining the human connection that drives true engagement.

In Chapter 10, "Your Dash," we'll explore how your unique journey — the experiences, challenges, and triumphs that have shaped you —

contributes to your distinctive communication voice. I'll share insights from my own dash that have informed my approach to communication and help you recognize how your past experiences can become powerful assets in your communication future.

>  **TRUTH BOMB**
>
> We fear what we don't understand, and when we fear what we don't understand, we automatically reject it.

Organizations exhaust so much invaluable time and energy on things they're not going to solve, fix, or change, which takes away from where they can actually make a measurable, tangible impact. As a leader, be willing to accept that not everyone is going to agree. Not everyone is going to want to comply. You have to accept that reality and be okay with them organically removing themselves from the organization.

These final chapters provide your roadmap for creating communication practices that don't just serve you today, but continue delivering value throughout your leadership journey. Because the voice you develop today — real, values-driven, and uniquely yours — becomes the foundation for your enduring impact tomorrow.

Chapter 9
Sustainability and Resilience

"If you are lucky enough to be someone's employer, then you have a moral obligation to make sure people do look forward to coming to work in the morning."

–John Mackey, Co-Founder and Former CEO, Whole Foods Market

When I talk about "sustainability," I'm not talking about going green or saving the planet. I'm talking about creating communication approaches that actually stick — that keep working for you whether markets crash, new technology disrupts everything, or workplace culture does another 180 (because you know any of those things could happen in the next six months).

Here's what I've learned after decades of coaching leaders: sustainable communication comes down to four things:

1. Your messaging has to align with what you actually value, not what sounds good in a meeting.
2. You need balance between when to listen and when to speak up.
3. You've got to create systems that keep improving themselves.
4. And you have to be smart about where you spend your communication energy.

When you get this right — when your words match your values and you're not exhausting yourself trying to be heard in every conversation — that's when you build the kind of influence that lasts. I've seen organizations completely transform just by getting this foundation solid. The difference shows up everywhere: teams move faster, ideas flow better, and yes, the numbers improve.

Look, we're living through constant change. What worked last year might be useless next month. That's why this chapter matters. We'll get into how to build communication practices that bend without breaking, how to save your energy for the moments that count, and how to stay genuinely connected to people even when everything's going digital.

The leaders who dominate long-term? They're the ones who figure this out. They build communication that's strong enough to weather any storm while keeping the trust and relationships that actually matter.

Building Sustainable Leadership Practices

Sustainable leadership can be about developing an existing approach that has worked for you. In addition to that, consider developing adaptable communication habits that serve you regardless of what tomorrow brings.

THE FOUR PILLARS OF SUSTAINABLE LEADERSHIP COMMUNICATION

Sustainable leadership communication rests on four essential pillars:

1. Alignment Between Values and Messaging

When your communication reflects your authentic values, it creates consistency that builds trust over time. This alignment is about what rings true, and it connects directly back to the leadership assessment we discussed in Chapter 5.

Remember when I explored the different leadership styles and asked you to honestly evaluate your approach? This is where that self-awareness pays dividends. If you discovered in Chapter 5 that you tend to be more directive than collaborative, or more task-focused than people-focused, that insight becomes crucial here. The leaders with sustainable communication practices don't try to force themselves into communication styles that conflict with their natural approach. They find ways to express their authentic values *through* their preferred style.

Great news! Truth bombs don't expire. When you speak from genuine conviction rather than temporary convenience, your message has staying power that transcends changing circumstances.

I worked with a healthcare executive who struggled with team engagement despite regular communication efforts. The worst part? All of her effort was burning her out. The breakthrough came when we identified the misalignment between her stated values of collaboration and innovation and her highly directive communication approach. She had been trying to sound collaborative while maintaining a command-and-control style. That wasn't working for her or her team. Once her messaging and delivery aligned with her actual values — she genuinely valued getting results through people, not despite them — her leadership impact became sustainable rather than constantly requiring reinforcement.

The key isn't changing who you are; it's communicating *from* who you are. When you're "the only one in the room," this becomes your differentiating advantage. Others may try to conform to what they think leadership should sound like, but your willingness to lead from your genuine values creates the kind of consistency that builds lasting influence.

2. Communication Balance

Leaders who master sustainability and resilience maintain balance across several crucial dimensions:

- **Listening vs. Speaking:** Creating space for input balanced with providing clear direction.
- **Transparency vs. Discretion:** Sharing context while respecting confidentiality.
- **Consistency vs. Adaptability:** Maintaining core principles while adjusting the approach to the circumstances.

This balance is about making deliberate choices based on what each situation requires (not simply splitting the difference) while maintaining a strong leadership presence.

3. Systems That Improve Themselves

Sustainable communication creates cycles of input that continuously improve both the message and the system itself. Think of it like a well-designed learning engine — the more information flows through it, the more refined and effective it becomes.

Too many organizations treat communication as a one-way broadcast system: leaders send messages, employees receive them, end of story. But sustainable communication works more like a conversation that never really ends. Each interaction provides data that makes the next interaction more effective.

Strong communication systems have these characteristics:

- Multiple accessible channels for different communication preferences
- Clear expectations about response timelines
- Regular assessment of effectiveness
- Mechanisms to capture insights and implement improvements

WHEN "IGNORED" REALLY MEANS "WRONG CHANNEL"

A client reached out to me recently with a frustration I hear all too often: "DT, I feel like when I'm communicating, I'm being ignored."

She had just attended a national conference for her sorority and was genuinely enthusiastic about what she would gain from the networking opportunities and sisterhood connections. On day one, she met a woman who seemed equally engaged in their conversation. They had a great connection, exchanged contact information — email, LinkedIn, phone numbers — the whole nine yards.

But here's where things went sideways. Over the following days of the conference, she wasn't able to reconnect with this woman despite several attempts. No problem, she thought. She was adamant about sending a follow-up email as soon as she got home (remember my rule: wait no more than 48 hours!).

She did exactly that. She crafted what she felt was a thoughtful message and sent it off.

Radio silence. No response.

After two weeks of wondering what went wrong, she called me. "DT, what am I doing wrong?"

I asked her a simple question: "What communication mechanism did you use?"

"Email," she replied.

Then I asked the question that changed everything: "Did you ask her what would be the best way to get in touch with her?"

This is where we put false meanings on these things. We assume everyone communicates the way we do, and when they don't respond, we make it about us. We tell ourselves stories: "She must not have liked me." "I said something wrong." "She's too important to respond to me."

But here's what I would have done differently. First, remember that you can't expect you from others. Not everyone checks email regularly or prioritizes it the way you might. Second, when someone gives you multiple ways to connect, use that information strategically.

I suggested she try a different approach. Instead of just email, send her a note through every channel she'd provided: call her, text her, leave a direct message on LinkedIn.

Guess what happened? She received a response within hours via social media. The woman apologized and explained that she rarely checks email but is very active on LinkedIn messaging.

The lesson? Sometimes what feels like rejection is simply a communication mismatch. Before you assume you're being ignored, make sure you're speaking their language. And of course, ask what communication channels people prefer to use. This will save you a lot of headaches, believe me!

4. Energy Conservation

This might sound unexpected, but sustainable communication requires energy management. Many leaders exhaust themselves by overcommunicating in low-impact ways while underinvesting in high-impact opportunities.

Consider your communication energy as a precious resource. Allocate it strategically by:

- Evaluating the return on investment (ROI) of different communication channels and formats.
- Identifying which topics genuinely require your voice.
- Creating systems that amplify your key messages without requiring constant repetition.
- Building recovery time into your communication rhythm.
- Knowing what your audience needs to hear and when.

Technical proficiency gets you in the game, and sustainability determines how long you stay in it. The most effective leaders are deliberate energy investors who create lasting impact through thoughtful communication choices. This is something that I personally had to learn the hard way.

If you were to ask my clients and colleagues to describe me in one word, many would say "energy." I've always been the person who shows up fully—passionate, vocal, and ready to contribute. For years, I thought this was my greatest professional asset.

During my time at Ironwood, I prided myself on being perpetually available. I responded to emails within minutes, attended every meeting I was invited to, and made sure to speak up in each one.

My philosophy was simple: it's better to overcommunicate than undercommunicate. I believed my high energy and constant input were what made me valuable. And they certainly did build a lot of social capital for me.

When I moved to Stonehaven to work on a massive Enterprise Resource Planning (ERP) implementation project, I doubled down on this approach. I was putting in 15-hour days, spending 9–10 hours in meetings every day, and making sure my voice was heard in every conversation. If there was a meeting, I was there. If there was a discussion, I was contributing. I thought I was being inspirational and making myself indispensable.

Then I hit a wall — both emotionally and physically.

I started noticing that my messaging felt repetitive, even to me. In conversations where I used to see engaged faces, I was seeing polite but distant expressions. Leaders who once sought my input seemed to be engaging with me less.

That's when one of my peers pulled me aside with a comment that stopped me cold: "DT, I hear you — and I hear you a lot — but sometimes I'm not sure what you're actually saying."

Here I was, someone who eats, sleeps, and breathes communication, being told that my communication wasn't effective. It forced me to take a step back and completely reevaluate my approach.

I regrouped around what I know and started treating communication like currency, asking myself where my voice really moved the needle. Was I amplifying important messages, or just adding noise? Before joining every meeting, I asked: Who else will be in this room? Where can I actually make a difference?

I began recording myself during practice sessions, becoming mindful of how long it took me to make a point. I started listening more and soliciting honest input from colleagues: "When I speak or present, what are you gaining from what I'm saying?"

This exploration in self-awareness was eye-opening. While my energy was appreciated, my impact had become diluted by overuse.

It's quite alright to have high energy and be passionate about communication. But I learned to ask myself three critical questions:

- What did I give in this interaction?
- What did others gain?
- Do I need to recharge my energy or recalibrate my approach?

The transformation was remarkable. I was speaking less, but I was being heard more. Colleagues were leaning in when I contributed instead of mentally checking out. My words carried more weight because they were intentional rather than constant.

This experience taught me that self-awareness isn't about changing who you are (I will always be extroverted and high-energy!). It's about making sure your energy matters. Again, the leaders who last aren't necessarily the loudest ones in the room; they're the most deliberate.

Creating Sustainable Communication Cultures

While individuals can adopt sustainable practices, creating organization-wide sustainability requires cultural shifts that touch every level. Here's how to build communication cultures that sustain excellence over time.

FROM REACTIVE TO PROACTIVE COMMUNICATION

Reactive communication cultures respond to problems after they emerge, often through crisis management and damage control. Proactive cultures anticipate information needs and create systems that prevent communication breakdowns before they occur.

The shift requires developing:

Forward-Looking Communication Calendars

Rather than waiting until information becomes urgent, sustainable cultures plan communication cadences that align with organizational rhythms. They anticipate when stakeholders will need context, updates, and direction, then deliver proactively rather than reactively.

Information Ecosystem Management

Instead of treating each communication as an isolated event, sustainable cultures create interconnected information ecosystems where messages build on each other, creating comprehensive understanding over time.

This ecosystem approach means:

- Considering how messages connect to previous communications;
- Creating clear pathways for information flow.
- Establishing reliable sources of truth that reduce confusion.
- Building redundancy for critical information without overwhelming repetition.

Recognition as Communication

In sustainable cultures, recognition communicates future priorities (rather than simply rewarding past behaviors). In other words, it focuses on those leading indicators (e.g., manager communication effectiveness scores, meeting effectiveness ratings, decision transparency ratings) we identified in the previous chapter. By consistently recognizing behaviors that align with organizational values, leaders reinforce what matters without constant directive communication.

BUILDING COMMUNICATION CAPACITY ACROSS THE ORGANIZATION

Sustainable communication isn't dependent on a few charismatic leaders or expert communicators. It develops distributed communication capacity throughout the organization.

This distributed approach includes:

Skills Development Beyond Traditional Training

Rather than relying solely on communication training programs, sustainable cultures build continuous learning into everyday operations through:

- Structured insights on communication effectiveness.
- Mentoring relationships that develop communication capabilities.
- Job rotations that expose people to different communication environments.
- Practical application opportunities that strengthen skills through experience.

Creating Communication Redundancy Without Repetition

Sustainable cultures ensure critical information reaches its destination through multiple channels without creating information overload. They achieve this balance by:

- Tailoring message format to the channel rather than duplicating identical content.
- Creating clear hierarchies of information importance.
- Establishing consistent patterns that make communication predictable and accessible.

Embedding Communication in Organizational Processes

Rather than treating communication as a separate activity, sustainable cultures integrate it into core business processes by:

- Building communication checkpoints into project workflows.
- Including communication effectiveness in performance evaluations.
- Measuring communication outcomes alongside operational results.
- Treating communication planning as essential to strategic implementation.

I've seen organizations transform their performance not by working harder or hiring different talent, but by creating sustainable communication cultures that maximize their existing capabilities. The difference shows up directly in operational efficiency, innovation capacity, and financial results.

Using Communication Skills to Stay Relevant in an AI-Driven World

Remember the AI-Human Skills Inventory I had you do back in Chapter 4? Well, that was just the tip of the iceberg (or crumb on the top of the muffin) when it comes to using your communication skills to stay relevant. Artificial intelligence is transforming how organizations communicate. This is a fact. Some fear it will replace human communication roles; others dismiss it as overhyped. Both perspectives miss the mark.

My prediction: AI won't replace *effective* communicators. But it will amplify the gap between those who master uniquely human communication capabilities and those who don't. What does this mean for you? Let's start finding out.

THE HUMAN COMMUNICATION ADVANTAGE

As AI becomes more sophisticated at generating content, analyzing data, and even mimicking conversation, your distinctively human communication abilities become more valuable, not less. These capabilities include:

Emotional Intelligence in Context

While AI can recognize emotional patterns, it cannot truly feel emotions or fully understand their context-specific nuances. Your ability to sense tension in a room, recognize unspoken concerns, or adjust your approach based on emotional cues remains uniquely human.

The leaders who thrive in an AI-augmented world will excel at:

- Reading emotional subtexts that AI misses.
- Navigating complex interpersonal dynamics.
- Communicating with genuine empathy, not algorithmic approximation.
- Building trust through authentic connection.

Creative Synthesis Across Domains

AI excels at pattern recognition within defined parameters, but struggles with the creative synthesis that produces truly original connections and insights. Your ability to draw unexpected parallels, apply insights across disparate fields, and communicate complex ideas through innovative frameworks will remain distinctively valuable.

Cultural Fluency and Adaptation

While AI can follow cultural rules, it cannot truly understand cultural contexts from lived experience. Your capacity to navigate cultural nuances, adapt communication appropriately across different contexts, and build bridges across cultural differences represents a sustainable advantage.

PARTNER WITH AI RATHER THAN COMPETE AGAINST IT

The most effective communicators will leverage it to enhance their distinctive human capabilities and create more sustainable communication practices. Here's how:

Automate to Elevate

Use AI to handle routine communication tasks, freeing your time and energy for high-value interactions where human connection matters most. This might include:

- Having AI draft initial content that you then refine with your unique voice and insight.

- Using AI to organize information before you apply human judgment to create meaningful narratives.
- Leveraging AI analysis to identify communication patterns, allowing you to focus on interpretation and application.

Focus on Your Highest-Value Communication Activities

As AI handles more routine communication, double down on the activities in which human connection creates the greatest value:

- Building relationships through authentic presence.
- Navigating complex emotional dynamics in high-stakes situations.
- Creating psychological safety in challenging conversations.
- Inspiring commitment through shared purpose and vision.

Continuously Develop Your Communication Signature

In Chapter 4, I also introduced the concept of your signature communication style. Here I want you to continue to develop your communication signature because this is what makes you recognizable and memorable. It's similar to how a physical signature is uniquely yours — your communication signature is the combination of:

1. Your unique voice and way of expressing ideas.
2. The consistent themes and frameworks you use.
3. The distinctive perspective you bring to conversations.
4. Your characteristic rhetorical devices, storytelling approach, or metaphors.
5. The values that consistently shine through in how you communicate.

Think of it like a personal brand for how you communicate. While anyone can learn basic communication skills, your communication signature is what sets you apart and makes your communication distinctly "you."

While AI can mimic general communication patterns, it cannot replicate your unique communication signature — the distinctive way you express ideas, build connections, and inspire action. Developing this signature becomes even more valuable as generic communication becomes increasingly automated. In fact, this is where AI can be a great asset. You can use it as a tool to analyze content you've written and develop your communication signature.

The leaders who thrive in an AI-driven future will be those who leverage technology while continuously developing the communication capabilities that remain distinctively human.

Leveraging Technology While Maintaining Humanity

Technology doesn't just include AI—it encompasses all the digital tools that have transformed how we connect and communicate. Using these tools effectively while maintaining genuine human connection represents one of the greatest leadership challenges of our time.

BEYOND DIGITAL PRESENCE TO DIGITAL CONNECTION

The shift to hybrid and remote work environments has made digital communication platforms essential. Yet many leaders mistake digital presence for digital connection.

True digital connection requires:

Intentional Presence

Physical presence alone doesn't create connection—bringing your full attention and authentic engagement does. This means:

- Minimizing multitasking during digital interactions.
- Creating space for relationship-building, not just transactional exchanges.
- Demonstrating active engagement through thoughtful responses.
- Being fully present rather than partially attentive.

Format-Appropriate Communication

Each digital platform has its strengths and limitations. Effective digital communicators adapt their approach to the format rather than using a one-size-fits-all approach. This includes:

- Matching message complexity to the channel's capabilities.
- Considering how different platforms affect message reception.
- Adjusting formality and tone to suit the medium.
- Recognizing when digital communication isn't sufficient.

Balancing Efficiency with Humanity

Digital tools create unprecedented efficiency, but overemphasizing this benefit can undermine human connection. Sustainable approaches balance efficiency with humanity by:

- Creating space for personal connection within digital interactions.
- Recognizing when relationship needs should take precedence over transactional efficiency.
- Using digital tools to enhance rather than replace human connection.
- Being deliberate about which communications deserve high-touch approaches.

AVOIDING DIGITAL DEPENDENCY

Technology should serve your communication objectives, not dictate them. Watch for these signs of unhealthy digital dependency:

Communication Narrowing

When organizations rely exclusively on a limited set of digital tools, they often lose communication richness and accessibility. Sustainable approaches maintain channel diversity, ensuring everyone can fully participate regardless of technological preferences or limitations.

Process Prioritization Over People

When digital processes become more important than the people they're meant to serve, communication effectiveness suffers. Watch for red flags indicating that your technology is driving your communication rather than supporting it.

Digital Doesn't Equal Connected

Digital tools can create an illusion of connection while actually allowing relationships to weaken through lack of meaningful engagement. Sustainable approaches include regular relationship strengthening through appropriate means, whether digital or in-person.

The most effective leaders put technology in its proper place. Rather than seeing it as either a savior or a threat, they see it as a tool that requires thoughtful application. They leverage its benefits while remaining firmly grounded in the human connections that ultimately drive organizational success.

Building Communication Resilience

Look, resilience isn't just about keeping your head above water when things get crazy — it's about coming out the other side stronger than when you went in. Communication resilience? That's what makes it possible. It's having practices that actually work when everything's falling apart around you.

THE FIVE ELEMENTS OF COMMUNICATION RESILIENCE

1. Cultural Preparation

Resilient organizations establish cultural foundations that serve them well in both normal operations and disruption:

- Creating psychological safety that encourages early problem identification.

- Building trust reserves through consistent transparency and follow-through.
- Establishing communication norms that remain stable even when circumstances change.
- Developing distributed communication capacity rather than relying on a few key voices.

2. Flexible Structure

Resilience requires structure; however, rigid processes break under pressure. Resilient communication systems provide:

- Clear frameworks that create consistency without excessive rigidity.
- Adaptable processes that can adjust to changing circumstances.
- Defined roles that provide clarity while allowing appropriate flexibility.
- Decision-making protocols that balance stability with agility.

3. Information Integrity

During disruption, information quality often deteriorates precisely when it matters most. Resilient communication maintains information integrity through:

- Clear source identification that helps people evaluate reliability.
- Transparent acknowledgment of what is known, unknown, and uncertain.
- Regular updates that prevent information vacuums.
- Established channels for correcting misinformation.

4. Recovery Mechanisms

Even the strongest communication systems experience failure. Resilient organizations establish mechanisms for rapid recovery:

- Regular assessment of communication effectiveness.
- Clear protocols for addressing communication breakdowns.

- Input systems that identify problems early.
- Learning practices that prevent recurring problems.

5. Relationship Sustainability

Perhaps most importantly, resilient communication maintains relationships through challenging circumstances by:

- Balancing task focus with relationship maintenance.
- Acknowledging the emotional impact of disruption.
- Creating space for authentic expression within appropriate boundaries.
- Demonstrating care through consistent presence and support.

PUTTING RESILIENCE INTO PRACTICE

Building communication resilience isn't a theoretical exercise — it requires deliberate, consistent action. The great news? Every exercise we've worked through in this book has been building toward this moment. From identifying your UVC in Chapter 3 to measuring what matters in Chapter 8, you've been developing the foundation for communication that can weather any storm.

Now it's time to put it all together:

Conduct Regular Resilience Assessments

Evaluate your organization's communication resilience by asking:

- How effectively would our communication systems function during significant disruption?
- Where are our single points of failure or vulnerability?
- What communication capabilities need strengthening to enhance our resilience?
- How well do our current practices build the trust and relationships needed for resilient response?

Practice Through Simulation

Don't wait for actual disruption to test your communication resilience. Create simulated scenarios you can play with on "sunny days" that allow you to:

- Practice communication under constrained circumstances.
- Identify weaknesses in current approaches.
- Build confidence in your resilience capabilities.
- Refine processes based on simulation outcomes.

Incorporate Lessons from Disruption

When you experience communication challenges, treat them as learning opportunities by:

- Conducting thorough after-action reviews.
- Identifying both what worked and what didn't.
- Implementing specific improvements based on lessons learned.
- Sharing insights across the organization to build collective resilience.

The organizations and leaders who dominate long-term? They're the ones who've figured out how to keep communicating effectively even when everything's going sideways, all while keeping intact the trust and relationships that actually matter.

Your Communication Legacy

As we conclude this chapter on sustainability and resilience, I want you to consider a question that has transformed how many of my clients approach their leadership communication:

What communication legacy are you creating?

Your communication choices today affect current operations, and they shape organizational patterns that may continue long after your tenure. The communication culture you build, the expectations you establish, and the capabilities you develop create an enduring imprint.

I believe my legacy is not just being a speaker, but also guiding and coaching others on how to use their voice with courage, compassion, and clarity. Whether I'm coaching a CEO for a high-stakes town hall or working with the public defender's office on building trust with clients, I've made it a mission to show people that communication is leadership.

I spoke at a summer internship kickoff for a company in Chicago where there were a number of young professionals trying to find their voice. What I shared with them is what I've always based my coaching on: Great leaders are great leaders because they're great communicators. Communication is how we connect with people — or not. It's how we build trust, and it's how we challenge adversity, injustice, and ambiguity. It's also how we create the future that we want.

A client recently asked for one of my favorite quotes when promoting me as a speaker. I immediately thought of Gandhi: "Be the change that you want to see in the world." That's what my legacy is, and that's what communication is all about.

I want to be remembered as someone who made people feel seen, who made people feel heard and powerful, even when they're "the only one in the room". Because I coached them and supported them on what they needed to say when it mattered the most. That's my legacy.

Consider:

- What communication principles will remain after you've moved on?
- How are you developing others' communication capabilities, not just your own?
- What systems are you building that will sustain effective communication beyond your personal influence?
- How will your communication approach be remembered and described?

The most sustainable communication impact embeds itself in organizational DNA through the patterns, expectations, and capabilities you establish.

When you view your communication through this legacy lens, short-term expedience often gives way to longer-term vision. Choices that might seem efficient today may undermine the sustainability you're working to build. Conversely, investments that appear costly now may create the foundation for lasting impact.

Your voice is indeed your most valuable asset. By developing sustainable practices and building resilience, you ensure that this asset continues to create value far beyond today's challenges and opportunities.

In our final chapter, we'll explore how to integrate everything we've discussed into your personal leadership journey, creating your unique path toward communication mastery that serves both your growth and your impact on others.

Chapter 10
Your Dash

> "For me, my role is about unleashing what people already have inside them that maybe is suppressed in most work environments."
>
> —Tony Hsieh, CEO, Zappos

I've spent years helping leaders transform their communication practices. However, I want to talk about something more fundamental, something that shapes every word you'll ever speak and every message you'll ever deliver.

Your dash.

You've probably seen it on a tombstone — that small horizontal line between birth and death dates, e.g., 1918–2012. It represents everything that happens in between. Your entire life condensed into a single mark.

Yes, communication is just like money — it's a critical tool that determines whether you thrive or merely survive. But understanding your dash, the journey that shapes your voice, is the foundation of truly transformative communication.

The Three Phases of Your Dash

Through my work with thousands of professionals, I've observed that most of us move through three distinct phases as we develop our voice. Understanding where you are in this progression can dramatically accelerate your growth as a communicator and leader.

PHASE 1: FORMATION

From the moment you enter this world until early adulthood, you're in a constant state of formation. You're absorbing messages about who you are, what you're capable of, and how you should communicate.

I've already shared a bit of my story with you, and honestly, it's hard for me to say this out loud (or in print); however, in an effort not to erase key information about my story, the formation phase for me began with abandonment. I entered the world without my biological parents and was adopted at five months. I didn't realize until much later how that early experience of rejection would shape my communication patterns — my need for external validation, my tendency to speak louder than necessary, my hunger for attention. Growing up in Evansville, IN, where I was the only one (or one of few) Black girls in my school, I learned that I was praised when I spoke "properly," but I was ridiculed if I expressed too much emotion. If I was louder than others, I was told I was being "too Black." So, "proper" speech became my armor. I made sure I was polished, controlled, and pleasant — just enough to be accepted, but never fully known or valued. I said what people wanted to hear, spoke only when I knew I was right. I did everything I could to make others comfortable, even though I was often not. It was a classic case of keeping myself small in order to fit in (see fitting in versus belonging in Chapter 3).

You likely entered the world with your own set of circumstances that created your initial programming. Perhaps you were told to "be seen and not heard." Maybe you were praised for perfectionism or punished for speaking up. These early messages created your communication baseline.

This formation phase includes what I affectionately call "making dumb decisions." I say this with zero judgment — we all do it. Whether it's choosing the wrong relationships, mishandling conflicts, or staying silent when we should speak up, these mistakes aren't failures. They're essential learning experiences.

The key to making this phase work for you instead of against you is self-awareness. Ask yourself:

- What early messages shaped how I communicate today?
- Which "dumb decisions" taught me the most valuable lessons about using my voice?
- What patterns formed during this period that no longer serve me?

Technical proficiency gets you in the game — but understanding your formative experiences determines how effectively you play.

PHASE 2: NAVIGATION

The second phase is what I call "lying in the bed you've made." You're dealing with the consequences of your formation — both the productive and unproductive patterns you've developed.

For me, this phase included becoming a mother twice before age 21, navigating toxic relationships, and experiencing domestic abuse. Professionally, I found myself in environments where I constantly overcompensated (being the loudest, the funniest, the most outgoing, outspeaking, outdebating). Because I hadn't yet learned to value my natural contribution, I felt that I always had to prove my worth. At the same time, I began to water down my ideas. Because I wanted to be seen as competent, I played it safe, convincing myself I was being collaborative when I was actually scared of being labeled "different." I kept saying "yes" to things I should have challenged. I didn't trust my own voice.

 **TRUTH BOMB**

The longer you let others define your voice, the harder it is to hear yourself.

If you've been paying attention, you've probably noticed that most of my lessons haven't come from books, they've come from bruises. And now I want to help others break this pattern. I learned the hard way, so you can learn from this book!

During this phase, many of us fall into some common communication traps:

The Competence Trap (which you're already familiar with): Getting promoted for your technical expertise, then getting stuck because you can't communicate effectively.
The Validation Trap: Seeking constant affirmation from others rather than developing your internal compass.

The Dependence Trap: Defining yourself primarily through relationships rather than your inherent value.

The Impression Trap: Focusing more on how you're perceived than on the substance of your message.

I'll never forget watching Denzel Washington in "American Gangster." There's a scene where his character, visibly frustrated with his team, says: "The loudest person in the room is the weakest person in the room." When I first heard that line, it didn't register deeply. Years later, it hit me like a revelation — I had been that person, compensating for insecurity with volume.

Don't get me wrong, the navigation phase isn't about perfection or "fixing" yourself. It's about becoming aware of the patterns you've developed and beginning to make conscious choices about which ones to keep and which to transform. It's about recognizing that your voice is one of your most valuable assets.

Ask yourself these questions to assess your navigation phase:

- In what situations do I fall back on unproductive communication patterns?
- What triggers my least effective communication behaviors?
- When do I feel most like me in my communication? What makes those moments different?

PHASE 3: COMPLETION

The final phase is what I call "completion," not in the sense that you stop growing, but more in the sense that you become complete with yourself. You no longer require external validation to know your worth. You understand that your voice matters, regardless of who agrees or disagrees.

In this phase, you realize that some relationships will naturally fall away, and that's not always a bad thing. Some people will choose to separate from you; you will choose to separate from others. The most important realization is that you cannot validate your existence based on what someone else thinks about you.

Happily, this is the phase I'm in now and it's the phase I support my clients in reaching as the Effective Communication Coach (realcommcoach.com). I realized that 10-year-old little Black girl from Evansville did have something to say. She simply needed someone to tell her that her voice was her superpower.

Now I tell myself, but here are the questions I wish I'd asked myself earlier:

- Who taught me how to use my voice? The first person I think of is my mom, Maurene. Then there was her mother, Agatha (Queen Aggie). There were also mentors who would remind me throughout my career.
- How am I showing up? How do I want to be showing up? Do I need to rewrite how I'm showing up?
- What unspoken rules did I previously absorb?

Once you ask yourself these questions, you'll know what you are made of. Then, you will start to rebuild. This phase is all about rebuilding. And it's about forgiveness.

Yes, there will be times when you are alone, but you will notice that you are not lonely. Your self-communication becomes your most powerful tool. Repeat these mantras whenever doubt creeps in:

"I forgive me."

"I forgive others."

"I have another day, and I get to choose how I show up."

 **TRUTH BOMB**

As a communication coach, my job isn't to teach greatness. Greatness isn't part of a curriculum. My job is to help you recognize the greatness already within you.

Like I said in the beginning, I'm not a trainer. Training is for animals at the zoo. So, if you've been paying people with the expectation that they'll teach you how to be great, that stops today!

Education comes in different formats. Yes, there's formal education (high school, college, certifications). But the true lessons that form us come from experience (but you can avoid the bruises!). When you think about how you communicate — whether on sunny days or stormy ones — it has *everything* to do with your experiences and nothing to do with registering for a four-year college degree.

The completion phase means accepting: "No matter where this thing called life takes me, this is the list of ingredients I'm given." It doesn't mean you can't add to the list or edit it. You never have to stop growing or improving. It means you're no longer pretending to be someone you're not. You no longer have to make the recipe others hand you. It's your kitchen. You get to make whatever you want!

Applying Your Dash to Leadership Communication

What we've really been talking about in this chapter (and throughout the book!) is personal development. Still, understanding your dash isn't merely personal development. It's professional intelligence. When you recognize how your earlier formation and navigation phases have shaped your voice, you gain tremendous power. It really is your career superpower!

USING YOUR VOICE AS YOUR MOST VALUABLE ASSET

Your voice is your most valuable asset. I've said it before, and I'm going to keep saying it. I may be a little bit biased, but your voice is perhaps even more valuable than your technical expertise. Everything you accomplish results from how effectively you use your voice. You use your voice by:

- Setting your daily intentions ("Today will be productive" versus "Today will be awful").
- Building trust with your team.
- Navigating conflict.
- Advocating for your ideas.
- Inspiring others to action.

When you understand your dash, you recognize that the way you use your voice is shaped by specific experiences. This awareness allows you to leverage strengths and address limitations.

For instance, if your formation phase taught you to avoid conflict, you might struggle with having difficult, but necessary, conversations. This doesn't have to be a setback. Once you recognize this pattern, you can develop specific strategies to address it rather than simply feeling inadequate.

BUILDING ORGANIC TRUST THROUGH REAL COMMUNICATION

When you use your voice to build relationships rather than to impress or control, something remarkable happens: organic trust and credibility naturally develop.

Trust isn't always a sunny day scenario. Sometimes you'll trust someone to be late or to underdeliver based on their pattern of behavior. True leadership comes into play when you can bring this to their attention: "I've noticed this is becoming a pattern that's negatively impacting our relationship. What do you need from me to support you so we can get back to delivering great work?"

Without your voice, these crucial conversations never happen. Problems become bigger, resentment builds, and performance suffers.

Your true voice becomes the catalyst for building genuine connections that withstand challenges.

FROM KNOWLEDGE TO WISDOM: THE JOURNEY BEYOND INFORMATION

As you progress through your dash, you move from acquiring knowledge to developing wisdom. Here's the distinction as I see it: Knowledge comes from formal education and technical training. Wisdom comes from experience, especially failure.

When I got my first major stage opportunity as the Effective Communication Coach (realcommcoach.com), I was so excited. This was my chance to really spread my brand, and I was ready to make the most of it. At this time, people were still spending days, hours, and weeks putting together PowerPoint presentations, and I was no exception. I practiced like my rent was due, like my life depended on it. And that was the problem.

I was so focused on being perfect that I forgot about the audience and being present for them. When I walked onto the stage, for whatever reason, my clicker didn't work. I freaked out because I had no way to advance my slides and I had created a dependency on my slides. Because I was freaked out, I forgot my talking points. I muddled my way through, but when I finished, I got some really basic applause. Even though I got a couple of claps, it felt to me like the room was totally silent.

When I saw the comments from the audience survey — because I always ask to see the results of audience surveys or solicit my own — I still remember to this day what one person said: "I felt like Denise wasn't there. And even when she was speaking, I felt like she was talking at us and not with us." I felt embarrassed, frustrated, and like I had wasted so much time (both my audience's and mine).

That's when I came up with the thought process: the only people that use scripts are actors. And nobody had come to this conference to see a Broadway musical. I took time to reflect and asked myself:

- Where did I go wrong?
- How did I get here?
- What do I need to do differently?

And you know what? I never made that mistake again.

This became a full circle moment for me. About two years later, I was invited back to speak by that same organization. After that presentation, I asked the organizer why she invited me back. She said, "Because I saw how disappointed and frustrated you were after the last time. Even when I gave you the feedback from the survey, you took it very well, but I saw how disappointed you were. Quite frankly, we've all been there, and I wanted to give you that second chance."

She went on to say, "I saw your growth, and you gave people exactly what they needed this time." I knew I had crushed it, not because I was trying to be perfect, but because I was being real.

I use this story in my coaching whenever I help people prepare for big presentations. I tell my clients: do not spend hours on a script. Do not spend hours on a single slide. Instead, prepare by creating the conditions you need to connect with your audience and be present.

This is my biggest lesson learned: communication is not about being perfect. It's not about having the perfect slides or the perfect words.

It's about connecting with your audience. People will remember how you made them feel through your personal stories and through your voice. Above all, they want to know that you're human.

When I started showing up as the real DT and focused on connecting with my audience instead of being perfectly scripted, it shifted everything. The next time you step out on stage, take a moment to pause. Speak from your heart. Ask questions of your audience.

Many professionals hit a ceiling because they continue pursuing knowledge without applying the wisdom their experiences have already provided. They attend another training, get another certification, read another book, looking outside for answers they already possess within.

Your communication approach reflects this distinction. Knowledge-based communication focuses on demonstrating expertise and appearing competent. Wisdom-based communication focuses on creating understanding and building connection.

The leader operating from wisdom doesn't need to be the loudest or most impressive person in the room. They know their value doesn't depend on constant external validation. This frees them to listen deeply, speak authentically, and lead with genuine presence rather than performance.

Embracing the Journey

Your dash is still being written. Whether you find yourself in the navigation or the completion phase, you have the opportunity to use your unique journey to develop a more powerful, authentic communication approach.

Remember:

1. **Your experiences aren't obstacles to effective communication—they're the foundation for it.** The challenges you've faced have given you perspective, resilience, and insights that nobody else possesses.
2. **Your voice is your most valuable asset.** Not just for presentations or meetings, but for every interaction that shapes your professional journey and impact.
3. **True communication mastery comes from self-awareness, not technical skill alone.** Understanding your dash—the experiences that shape you—gives you the power to communicate with power and impact.
4. **You cannot validate your existence based on what others think of you.** When you free yourself from the need for constant external validation, your communication becomes more powerful and genuine.
5. **The best is already in you.** I'm not here to teach greatness but to help bring out what's already there in my coaching clients.

As you continue developing your communication practice, remember that every phase of your dash contributes to your voice. The formation phase gave you perspective. The navigation phase taught you resilience. The completion phase offers you authenticity.

Your dash is the time between birth and death, but more than that, it's the journey that makes your voice uniquely valuable. Use it wisely.

Conclusion
Your Voice Your Legacy

Communication is just like money — it's a critical tool that determines whether you thrive or merely survive.

Throughout this book, we've explored how effective communication transforms not just careers, but entire organizations. We've seen how it builds cultures of belonging, drives breakthrough change, and creates sustainable impact that outlasts any individual leader.

As we conclude our journey together, I want to leave you with this fundamental truth: your voice — real, values-driven, and uniquely yours — is your most valuable asset. Not just for presentations or meetings, but for every interaction that shapes your professional journey and impact. There's a reason I keep repeating this. It's the most important takeaway from this entire book.

Whether you are an individual contributor, an aspiring leader, or a seasoned executive, your communication approach creates ripples that extend far beyond your immediate influence. When you bring transparency, vulnerability, and humanity to your interactions, you build the trust necessary for meaningful change. When you leverage your unique values and capabilities, you differentiate yourself in ways that technology can never replicate. And when you create cultures where every voice matters, you unlock potential that would otherwise remain dormant.

The journey isn't always easy. There will be times when you question whether speaking up is worth the risk, especially when you find that you are the only one in the room. There will be moments when old patterns tempt you back into silence or entice you to put on a mask that's not yours. In those moments, remember your dash — the journey that has shaped your unique perspective and given you wisdom that others don't possess.

As I've been reminding you throughout the book, technical proficiency gets you in the game, but your communication signature determines how far you'll go. Performance is just a fraction of what will take you to the next level in your career (remember the PIE Theory from Chapter 4). If you're not communicating your value — and making your contributions visible — someone else will happily take credit for your work.

As you move forward from these pages, I challenge you to:

1. **Use your voice intentionally** — not just when it's comfortable, but especially when it matters most.
2. **Build relationships before you need them** — investing in connection creates the foundation for everything else.
3. **Measure what matters** — track the impact of your communication on engagement, trust, and business outcomes.
4. **Leave a communication legacy** — consider how your approach shapes organizational patterns that will continue long after you've moved on.

The organizations and leaders who truly dominate their fields are the ones who create sustainable communication practices that allow them to adapt, evolve, and emerge stronger through disruption.

You have everything you need to begin this transformation today. Remember that your unique journey — with all its challenges, failures, and triumphs — has given you precisely the perspective needed to communicate with impact.

Your voice matters.

Your experience matters.

Your dash matters.

CONCLUSION

The world doesn't need more people who are technically proficient but disconnected (that's the definition of AI). It needs leaders who are professionally intelligent, who can build genuine human connection while delivering exceptional results, and who recognize that communication isn't a soft skill but the foundation of everything else. The world needs you, bringing your full human self to every conversation and using your voice to create the change you want to see.

I'm grateful that our paths have crossed through these pages. Now go make your voice heard. The world is waiting!

About the Author

Denise M. Thomas is the Founder and Owner of The Effective Communication Coach, a consultancy focused on transforming emerging and existing professionals into extraordinary leaders by mastering the art of effective communication.

With over 20 years of experience in Fortune 100 companies, including Toyota Motor Manufacturing, PepsiCo, General Electric, and Molson Coors, Denise has developed a unique ability to communicate across language, culture, and communication barriers. Throughout her corporate career, she often found herself as "the only one in the room," whether as the only Black woman, the youngest professional, or the only single parent. Rather than seeing these differences as obstacles, she transformed them into superpowers, developing communication approaches that allow her to connect with audiences of all kinds anywhere in the world.

Denise's journey is as powerful as her message. Adopted at five months old, she navigated early experiences of belonging and identity that shaped her approach to human connection. Her personal path taught her that technical proficiency may get you in the game, but effective communication determines how far you'll go. This philosophy guides her work with organizations worldwide, from the NFL to Northwestern Mutual, from Tel Aviv to Cape Town.

As a certified Hogan Assessment Coach, Center of Exceptional Leadership 360 Feedback Coach, and E-Learning Trainer/Coach, Denise brings both formal and lived experience to her work. She has been recognized with multiple awards by the Milwaukee Business Journal, including Woman of Influence and Top 100 Power Brokers for five consecutive years. She received Milwaukee Magazine's "Women of Distinction" honor and BizStarts' "Inspiring Entrepreneur" award. The Milwaukee Times Newspaper acknowledged her with their "Excellence in Business" award.

Denise holds a degree in Business Management from Cardinal Stritch University and is a proud member of The Links Incorporated–Trinity (Dallas) Texas Chapter. Whether working with C-suite executives, emerging professionals, or global teams, she remains dedicated to one core belief: your voice is your most valuable asset.

In a world where communication is often treated as secondary, Denise shows her clients that it's actually the currency that determines whether you merely survive or truly thrive. Through this book, she shares the insights and proven approaches that have helped thousands transform their careers and organizations through the power of authentic, effective communication.

www.ingramcontent.com/pod-product-compliance
Lightning Source LLC
Chambersburg PA
CBHW070722240426
43673CB00003B/110